Rachel McConnell

LEADING CONTENT DESIGN

MW00629231

MORE FROM A BOOK APART

You Should Write a Book
Katel LeDû and Lisa Maria Marquis

Responsible JavaScript
Jeremy Wagner

SEO for Everyone
Rebekah Baggs and Chris Corak

Design for Safety
Eva PenzeyMoog

Voice Content and Usability
Preston So

Better Onboarding
Krystal Higgins

Sustainable Web Design
Tom Greenwood

Design for Cognitive Bias
David Dylan Thomas

Cross-Cultural Design
Senongo Akpem

Expressive Design Systems
Yesenia Perez-Cruz

Visit abookapart.com for our full list of titles.

Publisher: Jeffrey Zeldman
Designer: Jason Santa Maria
Executive director: Katel LeDû
Managing editor: Lisa Maria Marquis
Editors: Adaobi Obi Tulton, Susan Bond, Caren Litherland
Book producer: Ron Bilodeau

ISBN: 978-1-952616-13-6

A Book Apart
New York, New York
http://abookapart.com

10 9 8 7 6 5 4 3 2 1

TABLE OF CONTENTS

1   *Introduction*

4   CHAPTER 1
     Understanding Content Operations

16   CHAPTER 2
     Identifying Your Operational Needs

33   CHAPTER 3
     Building Capability

48   CHAPTER 4
     Process, Tools, and Workflows

70   CHAPTER 5
     Establishing Standards

89   CHAPTER 6
     Fostering Collaboration

110   CHAPTER 7
     Beyond the Team

133   *Conclusion*

134   *Acknowledgments*

135   *Resources*

137   *References*

138   *Index*

This book is dedicated to anyone on a mission to put content at the heart of design in their organization and beyond. Baby steps...

FOREWORD

THE PROMISE OF DESIGN is that it can make technology easier to use. But behind the scenes, it's not without its challenges. For many content design teams, challenges in collaboration and communication can create barriers to success—barriers that become even harder to surpass as teams scale. Silos, duplicate efforts, and a lack of coordination can undermine even the most individually skilled teams, leading to ineffective practices and weaker products.

These are the challenges that a focus on content operations can address head on. Operations is one of the most underappreciated aspects of running an organization. Strengthening the people, platforms, and processes behind your content design practice is crucial for good leadership.

Fortunately, you're reading this book, where Rachel McConnell generously shares practical and proven methods to adopt an operations mindset and promote better teamwork. Her lessons will help you and your team remove barriers, build advocacy and capability, and continuously grow.

Because how teams work is just as important as what they make.

—Kristin Skinner

INTRODUCTION

THE PAST FEW YEARS have seen digital content disciplines mature, and smart companies today recognize the value that content brings to experience design. But as teams grow, it can be difficult for content designers to stay focused on content creation without getting bogged down in the operational parts of the job, such as workflow, methodologies, and organizational alignment.

As leaders, it's our job to create the conditions that allow content designers to excel in their work—and that includes taking on these operational tasks for them. Yet, the operational side of leadership is often neglected.

I've worked in a variety of content roles, in both in-house and agency settings, and I've been in teams of one to a hundred. When I moved into a content operations role, I realized that all those teams had one thing in common: they focused on what was getting done, but never *how*. Rarely did anyone pay attention to improving the conditions in which teams delivered their work.

Of course, getting the work done is important. But a continual focus on delivery can prevent us from identifying better ways of working, forcing us to remain reactive and with little time to scale an effective and efficient content practice.

To lead impactfully, we need to stop, take a step back, and look for opportunities to streamline our work, improve our processes, and become more flexible and strategic. Addressing operations—a core part of content leadership—helps everyone work better together to achieve the business goals.

Whom is this book for?

Content leaders are often people-focused, which is great, because creating the right environment for their people to thrive in is why leaders exist. But fostering the right culture also depends on processes, tools, and systems—operational aspects that can hold a team back from delivering and implementing even the strongest content strategy.

I wrote this book for leaders of growing content design teams, whether you're leading your team around unexpected obstacles, through organizational change, or simply toward a better way of working. This book is especially for:

- **Operations managers who want smoother content delivery:** Maybe your role is specific to content, or maybe you cover operations for all design disciplines. Either way, you want help understanding what content ops is and how to get started.
- **Content leads who want to help their team thrive:** Whether you're a strategist, head of content, or design or experience lead, you're responsible for getting the most from content designers, UX writers, and content managers. You want help understanding the barriers for content creators and how to remove them.
- **Content design managers who want to scale their team effectively**: Perhaps your team is growing and you're worried about maintaining quality, or perhaps it has grown with raggedy edges and the inefficiencies are starting to emerge. You want to know how to create a consistent practice and optimize your team.

Your job title doesn't matter; what matters is that you want to maximize the impact of content design at your company. You've realized operations hasn't been a priority, and you're ready to give it the time and attention it deserves.

Throughout this book I refer to those who create product content as *content designers,* and those who manage content within a content management system (CMS) as *content managers.* There's a lot of overlap between content design and UX writing (in fact, some organizations use the terms interchangeably), and sometimes content strategists may be doing content design work. But in the absence of a common term, content design best describes the process of working from research to design to implementation.

While content operations might fall to one person from an accountability point of view, actually doing the work is a team sport. You'll need input from team members, other disciplines, and other key business functions. You'll need support from your peers, your leadership team, and your direct reports. And you'll need to reiterate the value of stepping back from the day-to-day delivery to reassess and fine-tune some of your team's existing practices. Taking other people on the journey with you is key to the success of your efforts.

What's in this book?

We'll start with a high-level overview of content operations to help you recognize potential barriers to good content work. I'll provide examples of the typical challenges faced by content designers and show you tools and techniques to help your team overcome them. Repeatable frameworks will provide your team with consistent ways of working and better visibility for the outcomes, leading to more successful content delivery.

I'll also offer practical advice to help teams make incremental improvements. Every team is different, and what you need help with right now will be different from your needs in a year's time. This book will get you thinking more about the operational side of leadership, with tactics you can use as they are, or adapt and evolve into your own solutions over time.

With all that in mind, let's delve into the details.

UNDERSTANDING CONTENT OPERATIONS

IF YOU'RE LEADING A GROWING TEAM, you know just how much of your job is about fixing things to help the team work effectively and consistently. I bet that in every team meeting you hear at least one content designer complain about something that's blocking their work. These blockers are usually related to people, processes, tools, or systems—in other words, the operational side of the work.

If these barriers aren't removed, content designers become frustrated and demotivated. I've seen content designers struggle to complete design tasks or waste hours of work because they didn't have the right tool or the right fonts installed. I've even seen content designers leave jobs because the team wasn't collaborative enough and they didn't have the support they needed to do their best work.

All of these issues are solvable if someone is thinking about operations. Without that focus, the team just muddles through. After all, content designers are busy and focused on product delivery, often across multiple product teams; who has time to fix things?

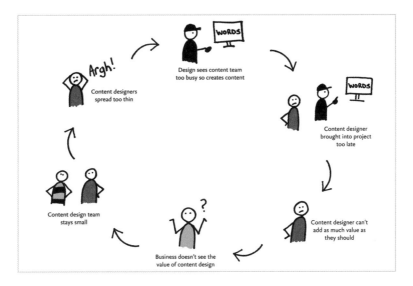

FIG 1.1: When content designers only do surface-level work, they can never fulfill their strategic potential or grow their practice.

THE CONTENT TRAP

You might be in a position where you've got a few content designers working across a number of product teams, and things seem to be going well. Or, you might have one or two content designers spread thinly across a large product design team, and although they're stretched, they seem to be coping.

But now ask yourself honestly: Are they really doing design work, or are they just operating at the surface level? It's common for content design teams to fall into what I call *the content trap* (**FIG 1.1**).

The content trap is a vicious cycle that keeps teams stuck doing low-impact work: when a content designer is part of multiple product teams, their focus is diluted, their time is reduced, and constant meetings and context-switching leaves them little headspace to add real value. The resulting shallow work exacerbates the view that content design "is just about the words," so there's no reason for the business to invest more resources into the team.

Meanwhile, the product designer can allocate all their time to a sprint, so they can take on all the strategic responsibility—and therefore the power. Content disciplines will never have equality in design teams when they physically can't invest the same amount of time in a project.

Add in dealing with clunky processes and inefficient ways of working, contending with multiple team demands (while lacking the context the product designers have), being brought in too late to influence design decisions, and dealing with many other business barriers, and you can see how content designers become even more stretched and demotivated. By continuing in this way, the content design team will never thrive and feel fulfilled by their work, and you'll lose talent as fast as you can hire it.

Watch out for these telltale signs that your team might be stuck in the content trap:

- **Content designers are always playing catch-up.** In an ideal world, content and product designers would work together to solve a problem: mapping out the key messages, content structure, and navigation before any high-fidelity design work even begins. But when "the content team is too busy," it's tempting for the product designers to race off and create designs on their own. When the content team finally gets to produce content, the designs don't work with the real content, or content decisions that can't be undone have already been made without the right input. The content designers are never involved at the point where their input can make a real difference.
- **You never get around to creating style guides or content frameworks.** The bigger the design team, the more important it becomes to have style guides, pattern libraries, and design systems to ensure consistency, quality, and autonomy. But when content teams are already too busy to keep up with the pace of work, they won't find time to create frameworks, let alone integrate them into a design system.

- **You have skill gaps you can't close.** A team heavily weighted in one area can become a self-fulfilling prophecy: the area with more weight—like product design—is perceived as having greater importance and will be given more resources. If content design is seen as less important, rather than as an equal partner to product design, it can be harder to convince leadership to provide budget for professional development, so capability improvements may stall.
- **Products are built with limited perspective.** A product team without equal weighting across functions isn't just lacking in critical skills—it's lacking in different perspectives, too. When these teams ideate alone, they miss more creative, innovative, and collaborative ways to solve problems. Incorporating multiple viewpoints also makes it easier to identify business opportunities and define research objectives.
- **The team is burned out.** Content designers often take on the burden of trying to solve these problems themselves. From explaining how a content perspective improves products and services to convincing product designers to involve them earlier, this continual education can leave the team exhausted.

If you've noticed any of these content-trap symptoms creeping into your team, it's probably time to stop, take stock, and consider how content operations can help move you toward doing more impactful work.

HOW CONTENT OPS CAN HELP

Content operations, or content ops, refers to the processes that enable consistent content design. Kristina Halvorson, coauthor of *Content Strategy for the Web*, defines it this way:

> Content ops supports the people and systems an organization needs to consistently deliver useful, usable content. It integrates and orchestrates all of the complex, moving parts of the content ecosystem.

This makes content ops a core part of content leadership. It lays the foundation for effective and efficient work, and frees up team members to think more strategically. While strategy is designed to deliver useful and usable content, many of us have learned (sometimes the hard way) that strategy doesn't simply get delivered from a keynote deck or a bunch of recommendations. Strategy relies on culture and momentum. Hilary Marsh, president and chief strategist for the Content Company, told me content operations is about building that culture:

> *[It's about] incorporating all of those policies, guidelines, and rules into the organization's ways of working—for example, putting rules into the CMS, building responsibilities into people's jobs, instituting regular training or internal communications, or establishing communities of practice.*

These kinds of activities are difficult for content designers to address when they're focused on customer-facing product work, but if they can be addressed, it will greatly simplify the content designers' work.

Content ops can mean many different kinds of activities depending on your organization. I see ops tasks as falling into five categories:

- **People tasks:**
  - Recruiting
  - Onboarding
  - Building collaboration within and across teams
  - Measuring engagement or team satisfaction
- **Capability tasks:**
  - Assessing team and individual skills
  - Capacity planning
  - Identifying skill gaps
  - Upskilling, training, and coaching
  - Facilitating crits or workshops

- **Process tasks:**
  - Establishing processes, workflows, and ways of working
  - Creating content frameworks and guidance
  - Defining standards and governance practices
  - Creating frameworks for testing and demonstrating success
- **Tools and systems tasks:**
  - Assessing tools and systems for suitability
  - Procuring new tools
  - Creating team tools and templates
  - Defining or building design system elements
- **Organizational alignment tasks:**
  - Managing budgets
  - Encouraging cross-functional work
  - Identifying efficiencies
  - Advocating for content practices
  - Demonstrating the business impact of content

It's unrealistic to expect content designers, whose focus is product work, to pick up these operational tasks and be able to have any impact. They need focused attention. It's also clear that the work can't simply fall to the team lead—people management alone could take up almost all of their time.

If a team really wants to move from reactive to strategic, content ops as its own role is a much better option. Between the team lead and an ops person (or people), these activities become much more manageable.

So how do you convince your leadership team to invest in content ops? The same way you'd sell a product initiative: by demonstrating the outcomes you'd achieve. I had a chat with product design leader Jonathon Colman, who said content teams can learn a lot from product management:

Content teams often draw inspiration from design teams when they think about their next steps forward in the organization. That's because those design teams are included in setting strategy and direction, invested in, and given focus to do their best work. But content teams would do far better if they looked at what those design teams are drawing their inspiration from:

product management (PM) teams. The foundations of business thinking and product strategy are essential for teams that want to be efficient, effective, and scale. The closer both content and design teams tack toward product, the more successful they'll be and the further they'll scale because they show the business that they're focused on what it cares about most: its success.

Product strategy is about helping products grow and become profitable. That's what we aim to do with content—scale efficiently and deliver return on investment. Content teams need to think less about their output and more about product outcomes. Demonstrating the value of content work on product outcomes will convince the business to invest further in content operations, because a well-rounded content team with focused roles will be able to solve business and customer problems much more effectively. Ops frees up content designers to go deeper into design work, define meaningful performance metrics, and produce a consistent, high-quality customer experience.

CONTENT OPS IN YOUR TEAM

If your team is struggling to focus on the operational side of content because it doesn't have capacity, then it's definitely worth making space for contents ops, whether as a standalone role or part of another role. Let's look at how content ops might fit into different kinds of team structures.

Teams without a content design lead

Sometimes content designers report to a design or UX lead and work across multiple product teams (FIG 1.2). Content responsibilities are distributed, and there's no dedicated content lead to take on any strategic or operational work. It's unlikely the design lead will have much experience with the unique challenges of scaling content design, so without support and advice from experienced content designers, content will struggle to make a big impact.

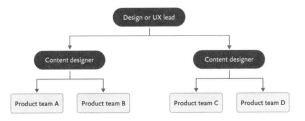

FIG 1.2: If an organization's content designers work across multiple product teams, the content designers might not work closely together every day.

In places with hub-and-spoke models (a centralized content function whose content designers work day-to-day embedded in product teams or on project work), the content team might also sit under a function such as marketing instead of design. There might be an overarching content strategy, but one that is probably more focused on marketing and communications, with little thought for how it translates into product design work. Again, in this team, it's likely the lead isn't familiar with the specifics of product design work or the barriers that arise for content designers.

In both of these team types, a content strategist or lead content designer might initially be more valuable than a dedicated ops person. Once they've set the content strategy for the product work, content ops could become the secondary focus to support implementation. Without a strategy or ops role, this team will remain reactive unless some of the content designers can take on ops activities alongside their design work.

Teams with a content design lead

Let's say you have a more mature model, with a lead who manages the discipline horizontally, and content designers who still sit within product teams (**FIG 1.3**). The lead may run crits, identify skill gaps, manage recruitment, and even establish best practices. As lead, they also have to coach and mentor their direct reports. If this person also needs to create content design systems or select new tools, you can see how their time can quickly become stretched.

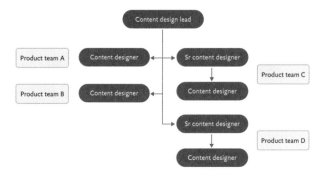

FIG 1.3: Even if a team with a content design lead and a clearly established hierarchy looks quite mature from the outside, it might not invest sufficient time in ops work.

This is the ideal circumstance in which to hire a content ops manager to take on these types of projects, especially as the team grows. If you wait until the team is bigger before thinking about the operational side, it will be too late; it's much harder to change behaviors and practices than it is to set good foundations from the start.

If this team can't hire a dedicated ops role, the content design lead should form an operations working group with the more senior content designers. Among them, they can invest a set amount of time each week—half a day, for example—when they can collectively work on ops activities.

Teams with strategic direction in place

Let's look at another model, similar to the previous one, but where they also have a content manager and content strategist in place (**FIG 1.4**). On such a robust team, operational activities could be distributed among the head of content, the content strategist, and the content manager.

However, as this team scales and needs to hire more content designers, that balance might become harder to maintain. Creating an operations role would free up the head of content to focus purely on the people side of leadership, allowing the con-

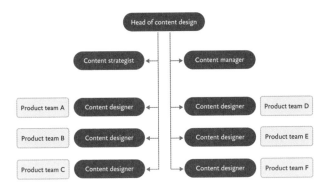

FIG 1.4: A team with multiple content leadership roles may be able to cover ops work among the team members.

tent strategist to focus on direction-setting and organizational alignment, while the content manager can focus on production workflow. The ops person can then take charge of things like design systems, tools, and capability improvements.

HOW STRATEGY AND OPERATIONS WORK TOGETHER

To be successful, a content team needs three areas of focus: direction (strategy), implementation (the design work itself), and enablement (ops). As we've just seen, depending on the size of the organization, different team members may share these responsibilities.

Content strategy and content ops in particular occupy complementary roles, and it can be hard to tell them apart. Think of it like this: if content strategy is the engine, then ops is the oil, making sure that all the strategic elements work together. Strategy is a plan of action to achieve an outcome, and ops is the enabler of that plan.

Let's look at various tasks that usually fall to content strategists and see how operations can help deliver them (**FIG 1.5**).

CONTENT RESPONSIBILITY	CONTENT STRATEGY TASK	CONTENT OPS TASK
Set direction	Understand business goals and user needs Set priorities for the content team	Facilitate workshops Align with other departments
Lay foundations	Establish brand voice and tone Define style guides Determine how content will support product strategy	Coordinate design system work Create content patterns or frameworks Determine guidance
Define team and roles	Identify who will do the work Determine skill gaps	Recruit team members Onboard new members Establish a community of practice Create skill assessments Organize or run training and coaching Create audit templates
Define workflows	Define how the work should be done Choose the necessary tools or processes	Assess existing tools and processes Procure new tools Streamline existing processes
Measure and maintain content	Define how success will be measured Set baselines and targets Define governance strategy	Create test frameworks Create case-study templates Share successes with the wider organization Create audit templates Manage platform users and permissions

FIG 1.5: Content responsibilities can be carried out more effectively when strategic and operational roles are clearly defined and avoid duplication or overlap.

Even if your team is collectively focused on content strategy, it's handy to break down the work into strategic and operational elements. Different people have different skills and experience, and harnessing everyone's skills enhances collaboration. Let's say you have a content designer who's passionate about copy consistency, and another who's very technical and good at systems thinking—they could partner on design system work, with one focusing on strategic content decisions, and the other focusing on structure, process, and implementation. With both strategy and ops roles, you can divide and conquer while helping the team understand what the strategy is and exactly how they're going to deliver it.

START WHERE YOU ARE

Content strategists and managers spend a lot of time defining and communicating strategy, but often forget about the enablers. When someone focuses on ops work, getting the design work done becomes so much simpler. You don't need any special skills to think operationally, just the willingness to ask questions, solve problems, and communicate—and these are skills most content designers have by the bucketload.

Whether or not your company's ready to invest in a specific role to focus on ops doesn't matter; there are plenty of ways to help your team scale efficiently and work more effectively. No matter your team's size or structure, it's worth identifying the biggest barriers to content work and laying strong foundations—and you can start by identifying your operational needs.

IDENTIFYING YOUR OPERATIONAL NEEDS

WHETHER YOU'RE ON AN established team that's just starting to think operationally or you're in the first dedicated ops role for your organization, you'll need to determine what to tackle first and how to integrate operations into your larger team dynamics.

I had a lightbulb moment in my first ops role when I realized all I had to do was put my design experience to use. By viewing the content team as a product itself, we can approach content ops as we would approach any other design project.

In a typical user-centered design process, we start with research to understand user needs (FIG 2.1). We then move on to define the problems to be solved and identify the opportunities. Next, we ideate solutions; then we prototype and test those solutions; and, finally, we measure their success. The design process is cyclical because as we learn from our solutions, we continue to iterate and improve until we get the desired outcomes.

We can use the design cycle to work out priority areas for content ops, collaboratively define solutions, and consider approaches for delivery.

FIG 2.1: A cyclical design process helps you design, build, learn, and iterate.

RESEARCH AND DISCOVERY

In the discovery phase, your aim is to uncover users' pain points. In this case, your users aren't the end customers but your internal teams. You'll need to observe, interview, and listen to your content team to uncover what is preventing them from doing their best work. You'll also want to talk to product designers, researchers, product managers, and wider stakeholders, such as the subject-matter experts or marketing teams who work alongside your content team.

You might already have some hunches about the problems you need to solve—but don't jump to conclusions. Begin a formal discovery process and listen carefully for the frustrations, blockers, and challenges within the content team. Beth Dunn, author of *Cultivating Content Design*, told me:

> *There's such a temptation to start offering solutions as soon as you can but it's vital to slow down, listen, and really get your hands around what the problem actually is. This is a design process as much as anything else, so doing deep discovery is the most important first step.*

Your research should uncover how teams are collaborating, what prevents people from doing good work, and what would enable them to work more efficiently. To find your answers, use familiar tactics like interviews, surveys, and job shadowing. I found these tactics also helped me build relationships, set the context for my role, and win support.

Interviews

The easiest way to start your research is with interviews—not only with content team members, but also with those who work closely with content designers or strategists. Book sessions with each person you wish to interview (thirty- to forty-five-minute blocks are usually easier to secure than an hour), and prepare to take notes or record your conversations (with their permission). Let the participants know their responses will remain anonymous; that will make it easier for them to open up and tell you what's really going on.

Questions you might ask include:

- How long have you worked here?
- Can you tell me about your role and what you do?
- How have things changed in the time you've been here?
- What do you spend the biggest percentage of your time doing?
- What are the biggest challenges facing your team?

- Has anyone tried to tackle these challenges before? What happened?
- What's working well with your current content design process?
- What's not working so well?
- How familiar are you with the concept of content ops?
- How do you think content ops can help you?
- If I could wave a magic wand and fix one thing about your team tomorrow, what would it be?

For non-content stakeholders, such as digital directors or other members of your executive team, find out what matters to them and ask them to help you understand more about their business strategy. This is also a good opportunity to gauge their perception of content design and how they think it should work. Questions might include:

- How do you define "content"?
- What does success look like for you in your role?
- What metrics is your team trying to improve?
- What do you think success looks like for content designers?
- Who has the final say on content here?
- How can the the content team better support you? Are there any shared goals we should work together on?

Capture as many verbatim quotes as possible, which will be useful for sharing your insights later. Pay attention to repeating themes that emerge when you ask people what they need help with. And don't be surprised if the folks you interview find these sessions therapeutic. People will inevitably have frustrations they want to vent, and letting them get it all out can also reveal key insights.

Time-tracking surveys

Another great way to uncover blockers for a team is to run a time-tracking survey, which tracks how individual team members spend their time during a given period. If your organization uses time-tracking software (such as Harvest), you can analyze its records; if not, you can track time in a spreadsheet. Start by creating a predefined task list for the team to pick from when they log their time. Make the tasks as granular as possible—a category such as "Meetings" might be too broad to get much insight, whereas listing out agile ceremonies, show-and-tell sessions, product reviews, and all-hands meetings will give you a more detailed picture. Think about all the possible tasks you might have around the meetings, too, such as "Preparing slides." Share your task list with a few trusted team members to check you haven't missed anything.

There are different ways to run this type of survey. You might decide to run it by job role (how are content designers versus product designers spending their time?) or by team (how many operational tasks are content designers doing themselves?). I've previously used this method to understand:

- How much time content designers and product designers were spending on collaborative design (the result: not enough, though interestingly, content designers spent more time collaborating than product designers)
- How much time team members were spending on operational tasks that I could take away from them (and thereby demonstrate the impact of ops on team efficiency)
- How much time designers were spending using various design tools
- How different product teams were spending their time, to get a picture of how more mature teams were working compared to newer ones

Ask participants to complete the survey over the course of at least two weeks. One week isn't enough—events like training, conferences, holidays, or leave can interfere with an average week.

Once you have your data, you'll need to analyze it and extract key insights. Your analysis will also highlight areas to delve into further. For example, if tasks like "resolving IT issues" or "tracking missing JIRA ticket information" are taking several hours a week, you might need to do more research to find out why.

Your survey results may also provide useful benchmarks when it comes to defining objectives for your team. For example, if your team only spends a couple of hours a week on collaborative design, you might set a target to double or triple this.

Job shadowing and meeting observation

Sometimes you need to observe design teams in their natural habitat to get a feel for how things are really going, day to day. One way to capture insights is to shadow a content designer for a few days. Job shadowing is a more time-intensive alternative to time-tracking, but it enables you to see firsthand how the content designer spends their time, what their biggest barriers and time-drains are, and how they're managing their workload. You may need to shadow a few content designers over a week or so to get a full view across the content team.

Another tactic is to observe meetings that you aren't usually part of. You can sit quietly in the corner and listen to conversations as they happen, taking notes about blockers, red flags, or anything that might point toward workflow problem areas. Again, you might need to sit in meetings across two or three teams over a period of a few weeks to identify clear themes. If you hear the same problems over and over again, these will be high-impact areas to focus on—and fixing them will help everyone work better.

Identifying your allies

As you progress with your research, it will become clear who feels most passionate about ops work and the areas they think you should focus on. While you don't want to commit to anything just yet (every stakeholder thinks their problem is the most important one!), take the opportunity to ask people whether they're keen to be involved in your design process. You'll need allies to help you implement your work and test out new processes, so it's good to involve them early.

Beth Dunn told me she often found frontline managers to be her biggest allies:

They're asked to do so much, and they get pulled in so many different directions that anything an ops person can offer them in terms of streamlining and amplifying the impact of how they work will tend to be so welcomed and embraced. They're amazing allies because they're willing to try things if they think it will help support their teams, and they're so close to the problem that they can funnel incredibly helpful feedback right to you in very tight loops.

Some of my key allies have been content design managers who don't have time themselves to resolve blockers and barriers. They're more than happy to support my work and be a cheerleader for content ops from the start—and in return I take them on the journey with me, gaining their input and feedback, and adapting to their ways of working.

Some stakeholders are resistant to change or to new processes and might not warm to your work. This often stems from fears that work will temporarily slow down (product managers seem to fear this one the most), that there will be more work to do (most often feared by individual contributors or ICs), or that autonomy or flexibility will be reduced. One way to alleviate these concerns is to explain the importance of ops, its impact on the team, and the long-term outcomes. If you already have allies, they can help make the case that the purpose of your work is to free content designers up to do what they love and what drives business value—the design work.

PROBLEM DEFINITION

Once you've completed your research, it's time to extract insights and define the most significant problems. Are there themes that keep coming up again and again? Map your notes, name your key themes, and summarize your findings. Alongside each observation, add two or three verbatim quotes from your research to back up your insights.

You may have a preferred way to present this information to your content and leadership teams. I've found that present-

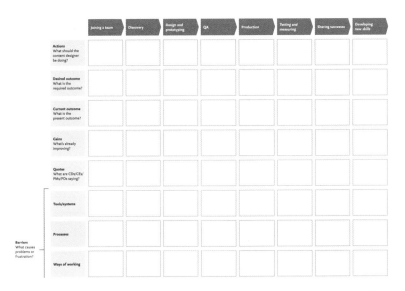

FIG 2.2: An experience map template can help you organize your insights—for yourself and for sharing with stakeholders.

ing observations, pain points, and opportunities in the form of an experience map (**FIG 2.2**) helps show what it's like to be a content designer on your team. My map includes a column for each stage of a content designer's job, from joining a new product team to developing their skills (developing skills happens throughout, but it's useful to capture themes in their own specific sections). This allows me to see which stage of a content designer's work has the biggest opportunity for improvement.

To create your own map, think about the type of work content designers are doing in your company. What are the specific stages of their work? Perhaps they aren't doing content production, but they have a hand-off stage where they share final designs with developers. Maybe "content team onboarding" is more appropriate for your team than "joining a product team."

Under each stage, create a *swim lane* to map your findings, including:

	Joining a team	Discovery	Design and prototyping
Actions What should the content designer be doing?	Understanding: • Key stakeholders • Roles and responsibilities • How to work with PD/PO/researchers	Taking part in discovery work/evaluative work	Codesigning with product designer
Desired outcome What is the required outcome?	Fully up to speed and ready to get started on work	CD contributes toward research objectives and outcomes and gets the same context as other team members	CD collaborates with other team members all the way through the design process
Current outcome What is the present outcome?	Confusion on best ways to work with PDs and stakeholders, not clear on product roadmap or priorities, limited Figma access	CD is often not involved with research and has to ask lots of questions to get the same background	CD is brought in when the PO or PD thinks they're needed, so CDs constrained by poor design decisions, can't add value

FIG 2.3: This detail of a completed experience map shows how discovery insights might map to different stages of the content designer's (CD's) journey.

- **Actions:** What should the content designer be doing?
- **Desired outcome:** What should success look like at this stage?
- **Current outcome:** What's actually happening at this stage?
- **Gains:** What work is already being done (if any) to improve the outcome?
- **Quotes:** What are content designers or their colleagues saying? Include verbatim quotations that bring the problem or opportunity to life.
- **Barriers:** What are the current problems or frustrations? It can be helpful to categorize these further under tools and systems, processes, ways of working, and capabilities.
- **Opportunities:** What else could be done to improve the outcome?

Next, it's time to populate your map (**FIG 2.3**). Capture any initial opportunities that jump out. You'll be able to add more in the next stage of the process.

This mapping process helps summarize the current outcomes and the core blockers for content designers in a way that's easy to share with the rest of the team. It also helps confirm or disprove your initial thoughts around the areas to focus on and frames the problem for ideation work.

IDEATION

Now that you've identified some ops problems, you need to start ideating solutions. Because ops work relies so much on collaboration, make sure you bring people with you on this journey as you come up with solutions; they'll be more invested, and you'll get better outcomes.

Workshop your solutions

Book a workshop with a cross section of the content team to help you come up with potential solutions. To prepare, look at the pain points you've outlined and turn them into ten to twelve "How Might We" questions; for example, "Lack of Figma skills" would be reframed as "How might we improve Figma skills?" It can be easy for teams to see what isn't working well, but harder for them to think positively about possible solutions. "How Might We" questions help shift people's perspectives toward problem-solving.

In the workshop, take two minutes per question to come up with opportunities to solve the issue. The ideas are meant to be quick-fire solutions, so no idea is bad at this stage. Ask participants to post as many ideas as they can before moving on to the next question (FIG 2.4).

Once you've discussed each idea, spend time *dot-voting* on the best options to implement. Ask the group to consider two factors for each solution:

- **Potential impact:** Which of the opportunities will have the greatest positive impact on the team? Think in terms of operational or customer outcomes: What will immediately

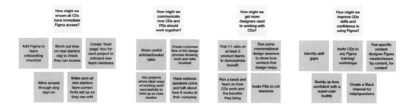

FIG 2.4: Use sticky notes to identify as many potential solutions for each "How Might We" question as possible.

improve efficiency or the efficacy of content? What will immediately improve designers' capabilities?

- **Amount of effort:** How much effort is needed to test ideas or bring them to fruition? What could you do right now? What needs further exploration or refinement, or more people or budget?

If you have a lot of ideas and need more investigation to work out feasibility, you may need to regroup later for this step. You may also need to discuss the proposed impact further.

You and your group might also decide to drop some solutions. But don't just drop all solutions that need more people, budget, or time—especially if they're high-impact. Your team can make the case for further investment to deliver these.

Once you're happy with your list of solutions, add them to the opportunities section on your experience map. You'll have a long list of potential solutions, and because the team came up with the ideas themselves, they'll be much keener to help implement them. That's more powerful than you saying, "I think we need to implement a peer review process."

Create a roadmap

The next step is to plot your solutions onto a roadmap—a great way to show your team, manager, and stakeholders what the ops focus should be for the next few months, and to highlight any key dependencies. Roadmapping can also demonstrate a clear pathway to long-term success through incremental change.

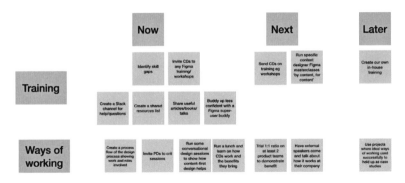

FIG 2.5: Group the ideas gathered from your "How Might We" session into time frames (top row) to create a roadmap for content ops, using themed swim lanes (left column) as needed.

Again, rally your content design team for a roadmapping workshop. Your goal is to identify and prioritize what you can do right now, which ideas might need to happen a bit further down the line, and which are longer-term strategic opportunities.

Start by creating three columns labeled "Now," "Next," and "Future." Take the solutions from your previous workshop and add them to the appropriate column based on the effort required to deliver each one (**FIG 2.5**). If you notice themes emerging around similar activities, create themed swim lanes to group them. If you notice dependent or linked activities, flag them. You may also notice solutions that need to be broken down into separate components; for example, "audit all content" might be divided into smaller audits over the course of several months.

Once the team is happy with the activities and their prioritization, create a more polished artifact to share with the wider content team (**FIG 2.6**). Keep the roadmap somewhere the team can see it, as a working document. Leave space to add more detail for activities that still need further scoping. Some activities might need to move or get deprioritized if more urgent projects arise, but the roadmap is a chance to demonstrate just how much scope there is for improvements across the team.

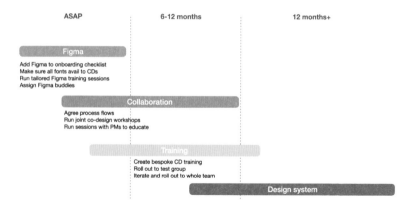

ASAP	6-12 months	12 months+

Figma
Add Figma to onboarding checklist
Make sure all fonts avail to CDs
Run tailored Figma training sessions
Assign Figma buddies

Collaboration
Agree process flows
Run joint co-design workshops
Run sessions with PMs to educate

Training
Create bespoke CD training
Roll out to test group
Iterate and roll out to whole team

Design system

FIG 2.6: A roadmap is a nice visual to communicate all the opportunities for content ops—but it's by no means final.

PROTOTYPE AND TEST

As with any type of design, we need to be sure our solutions work for everyone as intended before we commit. In this instance, *prototyping* means getting your ideas live and functional, even if they're minimal and not fully polished. A solution that works for one team might not work for another, but you won't know until you test it.

Let's take the example of a briefing template I created to help one team of content designers more accurately capture requirements for change requests. They helped me create it, they added it to their JIRA, and they were seeing improvements, so I assumed it would work for another team who needed similar help. The other team took one look at the template and gave me several reasons why it wasn't right for the kind of work they were doing. Their feedback enabled me to make tweaks to ensure it was suitable for them too.

When you can't roll out a whole new process or change everything in one go, a *minimum viable product* (MVP) allows you to start small and iterate as you learn. Not only that, MVPs let you build a few small success stories you can use to convince other teams of the benefits of ops. For example, starting small with a prototype might mean you create a basic online demo for Figma training to share with the team. If this is well received, you might create a more polished session with more content for onboarding new content designers, then iterate further and share more widely—perhaps with other content users in the business or beyond.

I've also used this method to test new ways of working. A colleague and I developed what we thought was a great new iteration of an existing process, which we hoped would improve team collaboration. We created a rough Mural template, gave the template to one product team, and asked them to test it and pull it to pieces. They came back with several suggested improvements, which we added for a test with another team. We went through this process a few times until we felt confident enough to turn our template into something more formal.

Prototyping also helps you understand which of your solutions just won't work and aren't worth investing further time in. I once built three "test" training modules in a learning management tool before realizing it wasn't quite the right tool for the team. The lost time was annoying, but at least I hadn't built the whole thing and invested money in the wrong solution. If you're exploring a new tool, build out a small proof of concept first to check that it suits your purpose.

MEASURING SUCCESS

Before implementing any changes, you'll need to define some benchmarks to measure the success of your solutions. Think of your content team as a product and consider the outcomes you're hoping for. What are the overarching business goals your ops work will contribute to? Is your business trying to make efficiency savings to reduce running costs, or does it want to improve the quality of customer outcomes?

Make sure your objectives align with your business strategy. Your understanding should come from your stakeholder interviews, but if you still have gaps in your knowledge, seek out your organizational goals and *key performance indicators (KPIs)* or

Business objective	Business needs	Content solutions	Potential success measures/results	
Increase efficiency	To simplify workflows	Implement new workflow with fewer checkpoints	Reduced content lead-times	Reduced editing resources
	Improve tools	Select a new CMS	Less time spent on content production	Less time spent in CMS

FIG 2.7: Just as you break out objectives and set success metrics for a product, you can use a similar approach for defining your ops goals and metrics.

key results. Your manager might already have some clear objectives for your ops work (such as delivery of a design system).

With this knowledge and your research insights, determine your ops initiatives and define how success can be measured (**FIG 2.7**). (You can do this activity as a team too—it's helpful to have more than one brain thinking about success metrics.)

1. Consider the opportunities you've uncovered that would help achieve your business objectives. For example, if the aim is to increase efficiency, this aligns with the content ops needed to simplify workflows and improve tools.
2. Next, look at the solutions your team has generated to answer this need—such as a new workflow or a new content management system. These are the initiatives outlined on your roadmap.
3. Identify what you could measure to demonstrate the impact of the proposed solutions.
4. Determine which of those metrics you could measure right now in order to establish a baseline. For example, if you've identified that a simpler workflow would reduce content lead times, make sure you note the current lead time. Your time-tracking survey should provide handy baseline metrics for these kinds of activities.

There are many measurements you might use to assess the effectiveness of your ops work:

- Time spent on tasks
- Production time
- Team sentiment (a simple weekly or monthly poll in your team Slack can gauge this)
- Team health survey scores
- Stakeholder satisfaction
- Skills assessment results
- Team retention (do content designers stay in your organization longer once their blockers have been removed?)
- Product team success (measured against the product objectives or results)
- Efficiency savings

If you're measuring efficiency savings, it's really powerful to calculate the return on investment your work will deliver, especially if you need to find a sponsor for the work. In her brilliant book *The Content Strategy Toolkit*, Meghan Casey lays out a simple process for assessing yearly efficiency savings for eliminating a given task:

- First, identify how many employees work on the task.
- Calculate the average time each employee spends on the task per week.
- Break down the average salary for those roles into a rough hourly rate.

Your calculation then becomes:

number of employees × *time spent on task* × *hourly rate*
× *52 weeks*

She recommends adding in any support time around the task that would go away too—for example, if the task needs a lot of IT support because the CMS is too glitchy for the task, factor that in. You'll end up with an approximate annual cost saving you can set as a target. That's as important to any business as incremental sales or increased profit.

I used this method to demonstrate the impact of automating some content production work to gain a sponsor for a tech project. While the benefit wasn't necessarily about reducing cost or team headcount, I was able to show that freeing up 50 percent of the team's time every week would allow them to focus on more impactful work.

Not all success will be measured in quantitative metrics. You might need to consider qualitative aspects like team sentiment, skill, or effectiveness. Freeing content designers up to take on more impactful tasks or contribute to strategy won't necessarily drive numerical results on their own, but it will contribute significantly to better customer outcomes. Some of the verbatim comments from your research can serve as useful baselines. Try running a similar round of interviews every six to twelve months to help track the qualitative effects of your ops work.

Whatever targets you're working toward, make sure you also set yourself a consistent time frame for checking in against them. You may need to follow the same planning cycle of your company, whether that's annual, monthly, or quarterly.

DESIGNING YOUR FUTURE

By approaching your content ops work like a product itself, you can better understand the problems to solve, generate potential solutions, and set clear success metrics to help you demonstrate impact later on.

When you define your opportunities in collaboration with the team, you'll help them buy into your work. And, with clear goals outlined, you can go into your ops work knowing exactly which areas to focus on and what you want to achieve. Not only that, but you can also use these targets to feed into personal objectives for anyone working on ops-related work—including you.

Whether you've identified process or tooling issues, capability or recruitment problems, or culture and relationship barriers, the rest of this book provides tips and tools for mitigating them. And as each challenge lifts, you'll find your content team working a little better, creating more effective content and thriving in their work.

3 BUILDING CAPABILITY

THE KEY TO AN EFFECTIVE content team is the people within it and how they work together. When you have a view of the content skills on and across your team, you can spot areas of strength as well as skill gaps. Knowing the shape of your team can help you make the right hiring decisions and ensure you build capability in the right places.

In this chapter, you'll learn how to create a framework to help you assess skills and identify training and development needs, and help you identify whom to hire. We'll also look at ideas for training and tips for creating a shared vision for your team—which is vital for team alignment. These things will help you grow capability from within and ensure you retain the talent you've nurtured.

ASSESSING INDIVIDUAL CAPABILITY

In your content ops capacity, you'll need to articulate expectations for your team's content roles and see how individual team members match up against them. Your organization may have defined role requirements for content designers, with different expectations based on their level; you may also have different expectations for individual contributors (ICs) versus management. If you don't have these, you'll need to define the expectations before you can assess your team.

Define role expectations

To assess your team, you'll first need to list everything someone in a given content role should be able to do. For this assessment you'll need to combine expectations from every level, from junior to senior. If you have a general job description for each level, that's a good starting point for this, and team managers can also provide input.

Break out your expectations into granular statements, so if a phrase in the job description for a content designer says "uses data and insights to articulate rationale and influence stakeholders," you might end up with:

- "extracts insights from data,"
- "makes data-informed decisions,"
- "provides clear rationale," and
- "influences stakeholders."

Once you've created statements for each level, group the statements into themes. These are your *skill areas*. You may end up with a combination of high-level skill areas that are common to anyone who works in your organization, such as "communication," and very craft-specific skills, such as "user-centered design." Keep the technical skills together. Your list may look something like this:

- Technical skills (i.e., the core craft skills for the job, such as "writing clear microcopy")
- Communication
- Facilitation and presentation
- Product and strategy development
- Collaboration
- Coaching and mentoring
- Data, analysis, and decision-making
- Advocacy

Data, analysis, and decision-making

Provides clear rationale for decisions ☐

Is comfortable using data to inform decisions ☐

Seeks out data to analyze performance and identify improvement opportunities ☐

Can extract key insights from data as a starting point for further exploratory work ☐

Provides key data to inform and influence ☐

Formulates and tests hypotheses to optimize content ☐

FIG 3.1: Turning your statements into a checklist will give you an easy assessment template.

Aim for at least six or seven skill areas; too few, and the categories will be too broad to be effective. These are the areas you'll assess your team against, and you want to get as much insight as possible.

Create your checklist

Once you have your list of expectations, you can create a checklist to assess your team's roles.

In each of your skill areas, list your grouped statements in order, from least experienced (a junior content designer may agree with the first two or three statements in the figure below) to most experienced (someone highly experienced will likely agree with almost all statements).

You can either use a tick box (which is ticked to agree with the statement) or a Likert scale with frequency ratings from 1 to 5 (with 1 being *never* and 5 being *all the time*). I used a tick box for this example (**FIG 3.1**).

As you create the checklist, make sure you refine the language to make it easier to complete. Aim to keep your skill areas as specific as possible, and check that you don't have any similar statements that fall into more than one skill area.

Conduct the assessment

Content design managers or team leads can conduct assessments in one of two ways:

- The content designer and manager can complete the assessment individually, then come together to compare notes and discuss.
- The content designer can complete the assessment on their own, then share and discuss with their manager.

When there's no content design manager or team lead, content designers can complete the assessments themselves and submit them to you or another nominated person for discussion.

While this exercise serves primarily to identify the skills that exist in the team and spot potential areas for development and training, it's also a great opportunity for the content designer and manager to evaluate whether the content designer is at the level they should be. Bear in mind that when a content designer completes this assessment, they're actually providing their own level of confidence in the various skill areas, which might not always reflect reality. Having both views will lead to more useful discussions.

Analyze the results

Once content designers and managers have completed the assessment and have a version they both agree with, it's time for you to review the results. By looking at all of your team's assessments together, you'll be able to spot where the most common development opportunities are and see where the team is tracking. Perhaps your team has a mostly senior skill level, but that's not reflected in their job titles, or maybe it's the inverse and you have a more junior team than you thought.

You and your team members may find a visualization of their results helpful to see where the biggest development areas are. The simplest method is to transfer the data into a small bar graph for each skill area, showing the number of boxes ticked

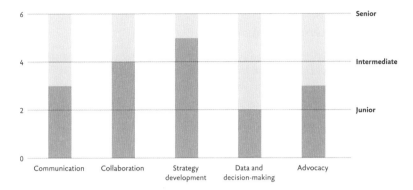

FIG 3.2: The light blue shows the highest potential score (assuming six statements in each skill area). The darker blue shows where this content designer is actually tracking.

---

versus the expectations for each role level (**FIG 3.2**). The difference between the two levels defines the potential individual development opportunities.

These results can help you identify what level to hire at if you're looking to bring more people onto your team. You can also use this assessment to identify job levels or benchmark skills for pay scales. Perhaps your team has been struggling to differentiate between a mid-level or senior content designer, or to determine who's ready to move into a more senior role. Assessments provide an objective way to evaluate this.

ASSESSING COLLECTIVE CAPABILITY

Individual assessments help you understand the competencies across your team, but it's also useful to look their content-specific skill sets as a group. This capability assessment shows you what technical skills you have versus the skills you actually need, helps you understand your team's strengths and opportunities, and facilitates the identification of the right people for the right projects.

Analyze content skills

To see the shape of your team, you'll need to create another skills list, this time focusing on content-specific technical skills. There's no need to create granular statements for this list. You can list as many skills as you like, but a good starting list for content-specific roles might include:

- UX writing
- Strategy
- Facilitation
- Prototyping

- SEO
- Accessibility
- Research
- Information architecture

For this assessment, use a Likert scale of 1-5, with 1 being *not at all confident* and 5 being *very confident*. Ask content team members to self-identify their confidence with each skill.

To analyze the results, plot each team member's results onto the same skills wheel, using a different color for each person (**FIG 3.3**). Place a dot at the level provided in the assessment on the corresponding skill spike of the wheel, then connect the dots to produce a shape.

When you look at the resulting shapes of all team members, you'll be able to quickly see where your team members' skill sets overlap and where there might be gaps. This visualization is useful when hiring, too—looking for someone with the missing skills can complement and upskill your existing team. This type of visual also helps other leaders understand why you might need to invest in a particular content area. Perhaps there's a big information architecture project coming up and you need to justify hiring someone for the role. It's a rigorous way to demonstrate current skill gaps.

Create an action plan

If you're helping teams assess capability, you'll also need to provide clear guidance for action planning. What can your team do once they're aware of the gaps? How do individuals develop their skill gaps? What can managers do to help them?

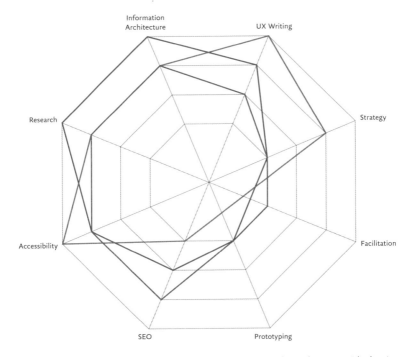

FIG 3.3: This hypothetical team has great skills on the more traditional content side, but is lacking when it comes to research, IA, and facilitation.

For clear skill gaps with existing team members, you could take several actions:

- **Individual plans:** Create a development plan for each individual with clear targets—whether that's formal training, reading particular books, job shadowing another team member, or taking a course. Usually, the content designer's manager creates this plan.
- **Group training:** Use coordinated training to close collective skill gaps. If your results show, for example, that research skills are low across the whole content team, heavily invest in training to build competency in this area. This activity falls nicely into ops.

- **Hiring:** Hire additional resources to close skill gaps. This might not just be for particular projects or to upskill the team; it could be because you've identified a gap in levels— for example, a lack of senior-level content designers.

When I carried out a similar skills assessment on one of my teams, we discovered a big gap in data analytics for content designers. We decided to build stronger relationships with our data team and to encourage the content team to use more data to inform their design work and define success metrics. We also developed simpler testing frameworks so more content designers could create hypotheses and manage A/B tests themselves.

If you use the assessment to provide a clear rationale for additional resources, make sure the resulting job descriptions are specific and emphasize the skill areas you need. You may even frame the interview around the specific skill area. I did just that when I needed to fill an information architecture role on my team. The hiring process took longer, but I got exactly the skills we needed, creating a more well-rounded team.

Share the results of your skills assessments with your leadership team. Be clear about the actions you're taking and the value that a well-rounded team (whose members can learn from one another) can bring to the business.

BUILD UP YOUR TEAM

Having a picture of the skills and shape of your team helps you consider how you might develop the people within your team, as well as the team itself. As your team scales, you can help your team lead make key decisions, such as what training to prioritize, when to expand the team, the skillsets to hire for, and even what the team's vision and guiding principles should be. When your team knows their strengths, they can decide what they want to be known for—and how they will get there.

Develop skillsets

Following the skills assessments, there might be obvious work-shops or training courses your team members need, and your rigor in highlighting these gaps should make it easier to secure training budget.

Reading and attending conferences and meetups (which help content designers meet peers they can learn from) will build team knowledge, and Slack communities are a great way to pick up tips and ask for help. But training doesn't always have to rely on more traditional, external methods—there are plenty of other things you might want to try with your team.

Buddy systems

Buddying a team member up with someone more experienced can help them grow a particular skill area or learn a new tool. Their buddy should be their go-to when they have questions or need help with a technique. This helps avoid the reluctance to ask questions ("the team looked so busy, I didn't want to be a pain") and the confusion around whom to go to with questions. I've found it particularly useful to buddy up a content designer with a product designer for training with tools like Figma.

Make sure the experienced buddy is happy (and equipped) to answer any questions they may get. If they prefer, they could set up a weekly Q&A session with their learning buddy to ensure regular opportunities for education and discussion.

Coaching

It's always great if you have senior team members who can take on the role of coaching more junior members. Coaching helps team members get through specific challenges, like pol-ishing their presentation skills or working through a particular design problem.

Coaching is quite introspective—it helps participants reflect on their own behavior and identify what they might need to adapt to improve. Determine who might be good at coaching (you may have identified this from your skills assessment) and in what area, and if they're interested, add their names to a list so you can call on them when opportunities arise.

Mentoring

Mentoring is a way of helping more junior team members build confidence. Having an experienced team member to bounce ideas off (or even just to vent to) is really valuable and also gets mentees used to showing vulnerability and asking for help when they need it.

I've found over the years that most mentees just want someone to validate how they're approaching a project or problem—they often will have come to the right conclusion by themselves, but they want to know if that's how I would have done it.

Skill sharing

If you have some team members with strong skills in an area where others are lacking, ask them if they'd mind running one-off skill-sharing sessions. Their manager may even be keen to build this into their personal development plan. Skill sharing could take the form of lunch-and-learns or 101 sessions, one-pager guides, one-on-one training, or even mini-workshops with the team. Record these sessions for anyone who can't attend.

A shared resource library

Even if you can't all be together in a physical space to access a shared library, creating a central resource list is a great way for the team to share books, articles, talks, and presentations they've learned from. Organize your list into clear categories so if someone's interested in improving a specific skill area, they can go directly to the relevant content.

Team tooling days

It's hard to get people's dedicated time to attend workshops or training, so it can be tempting to hand out quick guides to tools or just share links to team wikis. The problem is that to really learn how to get the most from tools, people need demonstrations and practice.

To encourage attendance at workshops and demos, I've found making a day of it works well. Building excitement with a "Figma day" or an "analytics day" means you can run a number of sessions for people at different levels, and they can decide which sessions to attend. Because it's a well-publicized event, content designers know others in their product team might attend, which alleviates the worry of missing out on key team activities. Making a day of it also helps build a community for the events and encourages discussion and sharing afterward.

Expand your team

If your skills assessment identified clear skill gaps you need to hire for, it's time to dust off those job ads and start to scale. While this book doesn't explicitly cover how to hire content designers (there are many articles and books about this, including my previous book, *Why You Need a Content Team and How to Build One*), a content ops perspective can help you identify *whom* you need to hire and *how* to grow.

Before adding to your team, it's worth taking time to reflect on *why* you need to grow, because this will determine how you approach your hiring:

- **Level gaps:** If you want more roles at a senior level to balance out your team, could any existing team members be suitable with the right coaching and support? If you're aiming to increase your junior roles, will your existing team have the capacity to support and grow new team members?
- **Skill gaps:** If you have capability gaps, what are they? Are you certain you can recruit specifically for these skills? LinkedIn searches on the key skills you need are a good place to start.
- **Too much work:** If there's more work but your team does have the skills, could you cover it by moving people around within your existing team? Look at product roadmaps to understand the work on the horizon, and make sure you

have good visibility of content designers' workloads to help you with capacity planning.

If you determine you *do* need to hire, ask a few more questions with your content lead or equivalent:

- What type of work will the new hires do? Are the responsibilities documented? This will be useful for creating your job description.
- What level do you need to hire at to complement your existing team? Is the structure or hierarchy already in place to support this? If not, how could you create it? If you have a flat structure, could you add any mid-senior levels to relieve some of the pressures from managers and provide growth opportunities for content designers?

If there's new work that needs to be done, include the project specifics in the job description. Maybe you need someone with app experience, or someone who has experience managing translations—calling out the specialties you need will save a lot of wasted time talking to the wrong applicants. If you don't have the right skills within your team, you might even want your new hire to run training sessions and share their knowledge—share this expectation with potential hires at the outset.

Create your content team vision

Having a shared vision for your content team is important. Often, product teams each have their own goals and objectives, so the only common goal your content designers have is the overall business goal—and even that could vary if they're working in different business areas.

Building your content team vision is useful for several reasons:

- **It creates a benchmark.** A common vision gives your team something to assess their work against. Managers can also use the vision as a point of reference for individual objective-setting: it's great if content designers have at least one personal objective that focuses on growing the content discipline and developing themselves. For example, if your team decides it wants to foster a learning culture, you could set objectives such as training or attending conferences, or knowledge sharing with the wider content community.

- **It helps establish ways of working.** A common vision reinforces the behaviors you want from your content designers and provides a basis for driving *how* your team works as much as *what* they deliver. If, for example, you want to make sure you're all collaborative, then the way someone achieves an outcome becomes as important as the outcome itself.
- **It fosters belonging.** When the team feels like they're shaping their mission together, they feel a better sense of ownership and belonging. It takes a collective effort to cultivate a strong team.
- **It improves advocacy.** Our main purpose as content designers is to make sure the user experience is the best it can be. But it's also worth spending time as a team to define what else you want to be known for by the wider business. This is important with a less-mature discipline, as we need to build our circle of advocates and increase our influence, and we can't do that unless we're proactive.

Your vision should be future-facing (hinting toward your desired end state), ambitious, and emotive, and it should illustrate your desired outcome. Set aside workshop time (or perhaps a team away-day) for content designers to get together and determine your team's vision—your North Star to aim toward (**FIG 3.4**). The following workshop steps combine tips from Julie Zhou's *The Making of a Manager* with exercises I've run with previous teams:

1. **North Star:** Ask your team to project themselves forward a couple of years—what are people saying about the team that shows how successful they've been? Ask them to sum this up in a simple statement. Share individual statements, look for patterns and similarities, and allow people to gently challenge each other's visions. You can refine them further with feedback, then dot-vote to find consensus. Or, you may

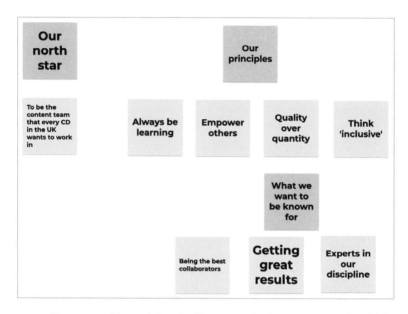

FIG 3.4: Your content vision workshop should generate a North Star statement, a list of skills your team is known for, and principles that demonstrate how you approach your work.

decide to combine elements from each statement to come up with a single statement everyone is happy with.

2. **Known skills:** Next, spend time as a team listing what your team is known for—your superpowers. What do other disciplines come to your team for help with? Are these the things you want to be known for, or are there other things the team is keen to add to that list? Agree on three or four of these known skills, and think about what actions you might take to become better known for them across the business. Maybe if you've been focusing on UX writing but actually want to be known as amazing workshop facilitators, your team could take some facilitation training and start hosting more workshops.

3. **Principles:** Ask everyone to list what they think are the core principles for how the team should work. This isn't about techniques for producing the work itself, but about

the foundational beliefs that drive the team. Vote on the top four or five that resonate the most with everyone.

4. **Put them all together:** For the final part of the workshop, decide whether you want to keep your vision statement and principles separate, or try to combine them into a single manifesto—a series of statements declaring your aims as a discipline. If you want to combine them, decide who will write the manifesto.

You might want to turn the final output into something that can live and breathe in your workspace, whether that's a poster, the cover page of your design system, or your Zoom background. It doesn't matter where it lives, as long as it's visible—something that provides a daily reminder to content designers of why they do what they do. Make sure you revisit it each year to check whether your ambitions are still relevant.

PLAYING TO YOUR TEAM'S STRENGTHS

When you're pitching a team, you need to play to individual strengths—putting the right people in the right places to help you win. And when team members feel motivated, supported, and happier in their work, you'll improve retention. Who wants to work somewhere that won't invest in their personal development?

By assessing the skills and shape of your team, and fostering a closer community, you'll have a clear view of the team's strengths and motivations. Having this picture gives you an edge—you'll understand the skills and perspectives on your team and know what to do to help them fulfill their potential. You might even identify people who have a natural flair for ops work and who'd like to work with you on the areas you're focusing on.

Once you have a vision for your team and a clear plan for skills development, you can turn your attention to the other things that help content designers get their work done: their processes and tools.

4 PROCESS, TOOLS, AND WORKFLOWS

MANY FACTORS CAN AFFECT a content team's ability to work effectively. Content designers may be slowed down by clunky workflows, tool limitations, and legacy processes. Without a holistic view of all of these, it's hard to identify exactly which parts need improvement.

While agile ways of working often favor individuals and interactions over processes and tools, they are all interconnected, so we can't shy away from exploring them. We need to understand those connections, starting with a high-level view of content design processes. Once we understand the processes, we can dig into the tools and relationships that influence and inform them—both within the product teams and with wider cross-functional teams—and uncover opportunities for better design work.

UNDERSTANDING THE CONTENT LANDSCAPE

In most organizations, the responsibility for content sits across many teams, from marketing and legal to design and brand. When we design content, the experience we create needs to fulfill or exceed the expectations our customers have of our brand, but we can only achieve this when our content feels integrated across their whole experience. This means we have to work with other teams to achieve consistency. But who are those teams, and how do we make sure we're working together in harmony?

Content creators can't afford to work in silos, because it creates a bad customer experience. Imagine, for example, a business where the call center, email writers, and app design team never speak to each other, and each channel gives customers different instructions for how to log into their account. This is just one of many possible points of failure across a business.

Content ops can help the team get to a place where everyone is aligned on the result, understands their role in content creation, and knows how to work with other content teams productively.

Ecosystem mapping

To understand the landscape your team is working in, first map out just what content is (and what it looks like) in your organization (FIG 4.1). This will give everyone a view of what content exists, who creates it, where that content lives, and what it's being used for. It's a great reminder for content designers to consider the wider context of their work and to stay close to other teams such as product marketing or social media.

To map the content, rally your content team (and, if possible, those working in other content roles such as marketing) and run a workshop to map your content ecosystem. This workshop may take up to two to three hours:

1. Start by agreeing on what sits at the center. It's the content most of your users will use regularly, likely your website or app.
2. Using sticky notes, list the content types that feed into that center channel. For example, do you have product descriptions or proposition messaging? Interactive content, like videos? Articles or blog posts? You might want to categorize broader content types, like "product content," "help

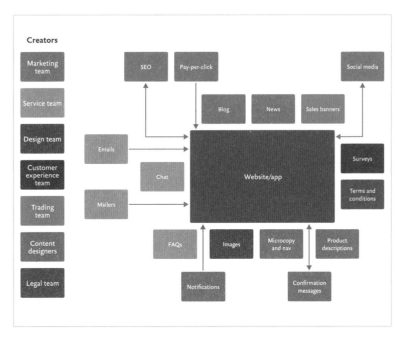

Creators

Marketing team	SEO	Pay-per-click	Social media
Service team		Blog	News	Sales banners
Design team	Emails			Surveys
Customer experience team	Chat	Website/app	Terms and conditions
Trading team	Mailers		
Content designers	FAQs	Images	Microcopy and nav	Product descriptions
Legal team	Notifications		Confirmation messages

FIG 4.1: An ecosystem map helps you understand how content connects within your organization and how many different teams are creating that content.

content," or "general company information," rather than go into granular detail.

3. Again, with sticky notes, list any other content your organization creates, such as sales emails, social media posts, or notifications. Include the content that gets pushed from your site, such as articles seeded in social media or emails triggered through a transaction. Add arrows to show the direction of travel; if there's content that pulls people to your site, but is also pushed out from your site, make sure you add arrows in both directions.

4. Identify which team currently creates each of the content types, and add those to your sticky notes. Try to group the sticky notes according to team. You might want to color-code them by team as you create your map.

RACI FOR NEW PRODUCT CONTENT

	Content design team	Marketing team	Service team	Product Managers	SME	CX	Legal	Trading	Test team	Design team
Provide new product information	R	C	C	A	C	I	I	R		I
Source images	R	I	R	C	I	I				A
Create copy	R/A	I	I	C	C	I		I		I
Check content accuracy	R	I	C	A		I	I	I		I
Test content with users	A	I	I	R	I	R		I		I
Brand review	R	A	I	I	I	I				I
Create meta-data	A	C								I
Legal review	R	I	I			R	A			I
Proof-read	A	R	I	I		I	I			I
Workflow Management	A	R	I	R		R	I	I		I
Final QA	R	I	R	R		I			A	
Publish	R	I	I	I		I	I	I		A
Measure effectiveness	A	R	I	R		C	I	I		I

FIG 4.2: This RACI for product content lists teams across the top and content tasks down the left side. You should complete a RACI for each type of content in your organization.

You can also identify which platforms are used to serve or host each type of content. This can get quite complex if your organization has many platforms—it is sometimes easier to map these separately.

Your ecosystem map should provide a clear, holistic view of the content that exists in your organization. It will be useful for showing stakeholders how extensive and far-reaching (and possibly fragmented) your content is. Also, if your map shows that teams in separate areas are producing similar content types, there might be opportunities for them to combine forces or work more closely together.

Identifying

Once you understand your ecosystem, it's time to learn more about the creation process for each type of content. Who's actually responsible for each type of content? Who needs to approve it, edit it, or just stay informed about it?

Often in big organizations, many people are responsible for creating content, but accountability is difficult to pinpoint. Or, teams that need to know about content changes—for example, a new offer or product feature—aren't kept informed.

A RACI chart (**FIG 4.2**) can help you identify role involvement for each type of content in your ecosystem. RACI stands for:

- **Responsible:** Those who do the work or make the decision
- **Accountable:** The person charged with delivering the content at a certain time and to the standard expected
- **Consulted:** Those who might need to provide input to the work
- **Informed:** Those who need to know about progress, changes, or status

You might find multiple people or teams end up in the responsible, consulted, or informed columns, but only one team or person should be accountable for each type of content. If you can't identify who's accountable, that's a problem to address.

You'll need to work with leadership teams to identify accountability. Show them your ecosystem and current RACI, and highlight the risks of no accountability—for example, inaccurate content could lead to legal challenges, or out-of-date pricing could cost the company money. Identify together what steps should be taken to assign accountability, and make sure the entire content team understands the changes. You might create a new RACI with clear accountabilities for each content type.

Accountability doesn't mean signing off on *every* piece of work—content designers should still be empowered to make the right decisions for users and the business. For example, content designers might be responsible for creating legal content with consultation from the legal team, with the product manager accountable for making sure the content is legible and gets surfaced at the right point in the user's journey. But while they're accountable, product managers shouldn't need to approve every piece of legal wording and can empower content designers to make decisions on a day-to-day basis.

Of course, there may be other occasions when the person accountable for the content *does* need to review and give approval. Make sure clear expectations are set around what type of content needs to be reviewed (and how often), so that nothing slips through the net. The workflow activity later in this chapter can help with this.

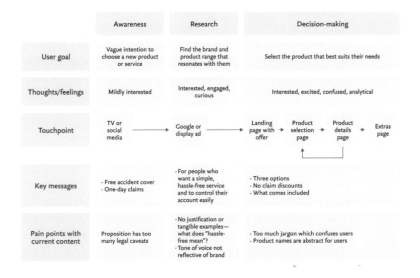

	Awareness	Research	Decision-making			
User goal	Vague intention to choose a new product or service	Find the brand and product range that resonates with them	Select the product that best suits their needs			
Thoughts/feelings	Mildly interested	Interested, engaged, curious	Interested, excited, confused, analytical			
Touchpoint	TV or social media →	Google or display ad →	Landing page with → offer	Product selection → page	Product details → page	Extras page
Key messages	- Free accident cover - One-day claims	- For people who want a simple, hassle-free service and to control their account easily	- Three options - No claim discounts - What comes included			
Pain points with current content	Proposition has too many legal caveats	- No justification or tangible examples— what does "hassle-free mean"? - Tone of voice not reflective of brand	- Too much jargon which confuses users - Product names are abstract for users			

FIG 4.3: This detail of a customer experience map highlights pain points caused by disconnects in content across the organization.

Customer experience mapping

What about how the content actually looks from a customer's point of view? Understanding the content experience helps all parties grasp the need for consistency through the user's journey, and how even content details such as feature naming can impact the experience.

A customer experience map (FIG 4.3) shows all the brand content a customer interacts with, bringing to life what the experience feels like for them. This activity also highlights any disconnect between content and those creating it and shows where there's room to improve collaboration. Bringing teams together to create a customer experience map is a great way to demonstrate the value of cross-functional working and reiterate that you're all moving toward the same goal.

Since you'll potentially be looking at a lot of content, you may need a day or two to map out everything (allow even more time if your participants are distributed). Include the people you identified as responsible or accountable for the content. Each team needs to understand how their content is or isn't working within the experience, and how collaborating with other teams will provide a more seamless and cohesive experience.

Use a very large wall space (or large virtual space) and ask people to bring examples of the content their team produces (display ads, emails, call center scripts, product pages, purchase journey screens, confirmation messages, etc.). They don't need to bring every single example, but the more you can map, the better.

Here's how to run these sessions:

1. Along the top of your space, add the stages of your customer journey. If your company doesn't already have these stages defined, you might need to define them together first. Make sure everyone's clear on what each stage means.
2. Down the side, add rows for the following:
   a) **The user's goal:** What are they trying to do?
   b) **Their thoughts and feelings:** What's their mindset at this stage?
   c) **Touchpoints:** Which content types do they interact with? (Allow enough space to add your content examples.)
   d) **Key messages:** What does the current content communicate?
   e) **Pain points:** What issues might the user face?
3. As a group, fill out the first four rows for each stage of the customer's experience. Include the examples that participants brought along.
4. Let the participants look through each example, noting any issues they spot with the content—disconnected messaging, inaccurate content, off-brand voice, etc.
5. Discuss the issues together, summarizing them as pain points in the bottom row. Brainstorm how each could be resolved and note any potential changes you might make to how you work. This part usually takes the most time.

6. At the end, assign any actions that come out of the discussion, such as setting up more regular check-ins, inviting other teams to product review sessions, or establishing a collaborative working group.

This session might be eye-opening for many of your content teams; it might highlight big issues to solve or flag duplication of effort, so be prepared for some meaty discussions. You might also want to create a more polished artifact, in case you need to walk other stakeholders through the complete map as rationale for any workflow changes.

Streamlining workflows

The final activity, geared toward understanding how content designers work with the other parties in their RACI, involves mapping out content workflows (**FIG 4.4**). This activity highlights opportunities to streamline existing processes. Run a workflow-mapping workshop for each type of content so you can keep it focused (the process for an article is likely to be very different than the process for a new feature design).

Here's how to run a workflow-mapping session:

1. Identify the content's starting point. Perhaps a request is received in the form of a brief, or a hypothesis comes out of some formative research.
2. Follow the content through each step in its design and development process until it goes live. Use sticky notes to map the step, the person responsible, and the time it takes.
3. There may be steps in the process that loop back—for example, content gets reviewed by a stakeholder, then goes back to the content designer for iteration. Make sure you mark these loops, too, and how long they take. Content production is rarely linear.
4. Once you've mapped your workflow, highlight any particular pain points—these could be steps that take a long time, steps that result in blockers, or steps that could be removed.

	Step 1	Step 2	Step 3	Step 4	Step 5	Step 6	Step 7
What	Content designed	Review	Revisions made	Legal review	Revisions made	Legal review	Designs built
Who	Content designer	Marketing	Content designer	Legal team	Content designer	Legal team	Content designer
Time frame	1 sprint	3 days	1-2 days	2-3 days	1 day	2-3 days	1 day

FIG 4.4: A workflow map shows how content gets created and by whom, as well as how long each task takes.

5. Now it's time to look for opportunities. For example, perhaps three stakeholders currently review the work separately; could they be brought together into one working session to speed up the process? Or perhaps designers are failing to collaborate, which results in them having to redo work once they receive the content. You'll likely come out with at least two or three opportunity areas.

It's helpful to turn your workflow map into a digital artifact showing the current process and suggested changes (FIG 4.5). This can help you influence anyone you need to bring on board with your plans to change parts of the process. Be sure to add the estimated time between each step in both your existing and proposed workflows so you can highlight the efficiency savings of moving to the new model.

Following the prototype model, test any new process with one or two content designers to get feedback before rolling out across the whole team. There could be good reasons your suggested improvements don't work or need tweaking. What works perfectly for one team might not work for another, so allowing teams to adapt or flex around the process is good—but you want to avoid them slipping back into old, inefficient ways of working, so check in with them regularly.

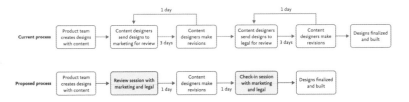

FIG 4.5: Current and proposed workflow maps, with changes highlighted in yellow so it's easy to see the benefits of workflow revisions.

Beth Dunn also tried this approach at Hubspot. She told me:

> As an ops person, I really had to find the balance between offering systemic solutions and giving teams the freedom to implement them (or not) in ways that were authentic to them as a team. I think in the end we ended up with much more useful approaches than we would have if we'd just sort of thrust things upon them.

Defining workflows collaboratively should make them much easier to adopt. But it's likely you'll still need other stakeholders to agree to any new process. Set up one-to-one time with them. Define the context of your role and your work—helping teams work more effectively and efficiently—and share the background of the workshop and input from team members before sharing the process flows. Bring their attention to particular blockers and how you think they can be solved. If they seem reluctant to change a process, remind them that it's a test with a clear review date in mind. This can help alleviate the fear of change.

ASSESSING TOOLS

If all your mapping work has identified that existing tooling could be slowing your teams down, it's time to rethink what they're using. The good news is you don't need to be an expert in the tools to understand whether they're right for the job. When it comes to procuring new tools, you can always partner with a superuser from the team. It's not cheating to ask for help—in fact, ops work relies on input from others.

Identifying tool opportunities

When I first joined my current role, I realized that while everyone on the team was using the same CMS to build out their content, they were all on different instances of it. It seemed impossible to wrap my head around the various CMS versions and their challenges.

Instead of trying to get to the bottom of the challenges myself, I formed a working group of content designers and CMS developers so that the content and development teams could work closer together, pool their knowledge, and identify improvement areas. This allowed the content team to share their frustrations directly with the dev team and, in turn, the developers could make sure any CMS changes met the designers' needs.

As well as opening lines of communication between content and dev teams, it became easier for everyone to discuss their pain points together. We included workshop time for this in our regular sessions. One useful activity was capturing the basic requirements for a CMS and identifying what was missing from their current instance, which highlighted areas of immediate action as well as some that needed further exploration.

To identify the improvements your tooling might need, first revisit your initial discovery work (from Chapter 2). If you captured a lot of pain points around tools, review your notes and see what you'd like to dig into further. A simple demo from a content designer of how they complete a common task can help clarify things. Ask them to show you how the problem impacts task completion and to specify the impact of the problem (for example, creating a new piece of content takes three hours instead of five minutes). Specificity will help you later: if you need senior sponsorship for tool changes, you'll be better able to demonstrate the business impact of any improvements. Remember, impact doesn't always have to be a cost saving—time saved on poor tooling is time that can be spent on higher-value work.

As a user I want to.....	Must	Should	Nice to have	Currently?
Create a new component	Y			Y
Name a component	Y			Y
Define a page URL	Y			Y
Duplicate an existing component	Y			Y
Add images to a component	Y			Y
Have images automatically resized (format) when they're added		Y		Y
Hyperlink images	Y			Y
Format headers	Y			Y
Include text formatting such as bullet points and subheaders	Y			Y
Add alt-text to images	Y			Y
Add metadata	Y			Y
Choose from defined font styles/sizes	Y			N
Have flexibility to choose the appropriate component layout	Y			Y
Add tagged URL/tracking to a component		Y		Y
Create categories		Y		Y
Assign a page to a category		Y		N
Generate related links for a page	Y			Y
Automatically generate related links for a page based on user's history			Y	Y
Create a master content component to be reused across multiple pages	Y			Y
Allow a content component to work as a single instance or as a master component	Y			N
Add social sharing links	Y			(Limited)
Integrate a data source (such as a pricing spreadsheet)	Y			N
Insert a video	Y			(Limited)
Embed an image or infographic	Y			Y
Insert media from an asset library	Y			Y
Integrate test tools to present different content to different users	Y			N
Embed a form tool such as typeform	Y			Y
Save a component as draft	Y			(Limited)

FIG 4.6: A spreadsheet can gather tool requirements, such as the must-have functionality for a CMS, and indicate whether or not the current tool actually meets the requirements.

Sometimes improvements to a tool won't be enough. If the tool isn't up to the task, you might need to change it completely. If that's the case, you'll need to understand what the right tool needs to do.

Identifying requirements

Start by gathering requirements for the type of tool you need to accomplish content tasks. Any new tool will probably need to benefit other teams as well, but in your role, you're responsible for making sure your content team has what they need to do their jobs effectively. Capturing their needs is your first step.

Bring together the content team for a half-day requirements workshop:

1. Capture all the tasks the team needs the tool to do. The tasks should be as granular as possible—for example, if you were assessing a CMS, you would differentiate "creating new content" from "editing existing content." Record this list either in a spreadsheet or with sticky notes on a wall.

2. Create four columns next to this list: "Must," "Should," "Nice to have," and "Currently?".
3. Go through each list item and capture the priority of each requirement. Be realistic, but also ruthless. Don't think about your current tool yet.
4. Once you've discussed each requirement, it's time to assess your current tool: go down the list again and assess whether your current tool does or doesn't provide that functionality. Capture this in the final column with "yes," "no," or "partially."

At the end of this workshop, you'll understand whether your current tool is fit for purpose, and you'll have the basic requirements to assess any new tool against (**FIG 4.6**). If one or two team members seem particularly passionate about the tooling or selecting a new one, ask them to work with you (or for you) to identify and assess alternative options.

Tool governance

As well as selecting the right tools to use for content production, you might want to define common standards and rules around how the tools are used. You'll need to work with your development team to configure any new platform, so it's worth defining this governance first.

Consider how the tool will be permissioned. To define users and permissions, sit down with your content lead, any other team leads who'll have access to the tools, and your dev team (if they'll need to configure the tool). Together, determine:

- Who will need access to the tool? What kind of access?
- How many licenses will you need? Will the tool allow you to regularly reassign licenses?
- How often will the users be reviewed?
- What's the process for adding and removing users? Who's responsible for removing users when they leave the business?

Don't forget your cross-functional content colleagues—for example, if you're considering or working with a headless CMS (allowing content to be repurposed in different places), complete a RACI with those other teams to determine who'll be accountable and responsible for creating, maintaining, and updating content in the CMS.

USING PROCESS TO INFLUENCE CHANGE

The organization of your content team—centralized, embedded within product teams, or somewhere in between—can affect everything from collaboration to prioritization. While organizational change is often beyond our control, we can use process to nudge ourselves toward the changes we want to see. We can optimize our tools, workflows, and even documentation to iron out some of the kinks in our organizational layers.

Create a briefing process

Content work can come into the team in very different ways. It may be the result of discovery research by a product team that's involving the content designer to create solutions. It may come from evaluative research, where content designers have defined some clear opportunity areas. At other times, it may simply reflect stakeholder requests to revise something (for example, proposition messaging). And any of this work could be communicated via a discussion, a JIRA ticket, or an email.

Very rarely is there a common format for intake, which makes it hard to prioritize tasks if you don't have content designers aligned to product teams. Content designers often have to start work without all the right information, which slows the process down. Remember that time-tracking survey from Chapter 2? It revealed that some content designers were spending up to half a day a week chasing down missing information!

Change/request owner	
Target audiences/users	
Reason for request (e.g. user insights, business needs)	
Briefly describe what's needed (the scope of this work)	
How will success be measured?	
Key messages to communicate	
Target launch date	
End date (if applicable)	
Marketing/SEO requirements if known (keywords, meta descriptions, tracking URLs, etc)	
Any legal requirements/T&Cs?	
Links to any relevant assets (e.g. images)	
Any additional info	

FIG 4.7: A content briefing template helps content teams capture all the information they might need to start working on a specific content request. It avoids jargon to keep things simple.

If this sounds like your team, one of the first things you can do is create a briefing process for new work that comes in from outside of the product team, such as marketing or legal requests. A simple briefing process can gather key information, clarify expectations, and prevent stakeholders from requesting their own solutions, instead nudging them to outline the user or business need they need to respond to. It also helps clarify the objective, purpose, or expected outcome for the request—details that are often missing from requests originating outside of the design team.

Too often, content requests are assumed to be "quick tasks" that are accepted by teams without real estimation work. But with a brief, a content designer can make a real assessment of the work involved, set clear expectations, and better manage their workload. The team can also prioritize more effectively, focusing on the high-impact work that helps advance business goals.

Decide within the content team who will triage incoming briefs; it could be the content lead or a group of content design managers who meet weekly to discuss the requests. If you have project or product managers, they can also help with this.

Your briefing template should include details like the problem to be solved, the expected outcome, the audience, applicable dates, legal requirements, and any other considerations that will affect the content (FIG 4.7). Keep your template as simple as possible and avoid design language that external stakeholders might not be familiar with. The brief should nudge them to carefully consider the need for new content and help them understand what goes into creating genuinely user-centered content.

As well as creating and distributing the template, explain the new briefing process to those responsible for bringing work into the team. Explain that you'd like to trial a more organized approach to help content designers provide quality output. Stress that you're looking for ways to work more effectively and efficiently, and to ensure content designers have the right information up front so they can accurately estimate how long the work will take. Present your proposed brief template and ask requestors to trial it for a couple of months to see how it improves both the quality of work and the speed of delivery.

Make content requests visible

Keeping a visible backlog of incoming work shows stakeholders just how much is on your team's plate, and how it's prioritized. When they understand more about your process and workload, they'll better appreciate lead times and hopefully reduce their side-of-desk requests. Or, as Torrey Podmajersky put it in *Strategic Writing for UX*:

By making content tasks visible, the team understands the work it takes for the UX content to advance the goals of engineering, design, and the organization, while it supports the person who will use it. In the process of doing the work, the UX content goes from being a source of pain to being valued.

Keeping requests visible can also highlight blockers. If the content designer doesn't have all they need to complete a task, this should be visibly flagged. I once walked a compliance team through a workload wall to show them how many content tasks in the "blocked" column depended on them. Once they'd seen the impact, they started helping us right away.

In *Writing Is Designing*, Michael Metts and Andy Welfle refer to this as *contagious transparency*, making the point that "transparency helps everyone understand your workflow and how they can help you."

Find a wall space or accessible digital space (such as a public Trello board) and create columns for "Backlog," "In progress," "Blocked," and "Done." As each request comes in, the triage team logs the work and assigns a content designer. If you're using project management software, they can create a ticket; if you're using a physical wall, an index card is perfect for this. The content designer can add their estimated time to the ticket.

Bring the content team together regularly (weekly at a minimum, but daily if you can) to review the work, move the tickets, and discuss key blockers. If you need to, bring stakeholders into these stand-up sessions to discuss blockers and capacity.

It's much easier to push back on requests when the team has a visible workload to point to. Sometimes saying no and being stricter on what you can and can't deliver will force additional hiring or better ways of working. There are also times when the team needs to focus on high-impact work and let the low-priority items go, even if that means the content doesn't get created by content designers. It's not easy saying no to things, but when a team is stretched, saying yes to everything will keep the team reactive and prevent them from doing more than just surface-level work.

Content element	Copy	Show if
<H1>	Your details	
<H2>	Please provide a few details about your claim	
<Image>	car.jpg	
<Body 1>	Make sure you have your licence number and payment details to hand.	
<H2>	Your car	
<Field label>	Registration number	
<Error message>	Enter your registration number to continue	Non entry
<Error message>	Hmm, we couldn't find that car, please try again	No match
<CTA 1>	Continue	

FIG 4.8: A simple copy doc can be a quick way to document content for development teams.

Standardize content hand-off

If your team works with development teams that aren't in-house, handing over designs and content for build can be a really tricky process. Some development teams will only work from copy documents that are separate from design files. This can mean a lot of discussions between content design and development, which takes time and complicates QA testing.

Creating a standardized template for copy allows content designers to simply copy and paste into a spreadsheet, which saves time and gives developers a guide to work from (FIG 4.8). The template should clearly outline the page's content elements and copy, alongside any rules (particularly important for form fields, error and validation messages, etc.). This is quicker to complete than writing out the copy in a Google Doc or Word document each time and reduces friction between developers and design teams, which in turn can speed up build time. It also provides clear documentation of content, which can be added to the task ticket so there's an audit trail, which is necessary for some organizations.

An even better idea for development, which avoids the need for documentation, is to explore a more strategic software solution that extracts the content from design files. This can be helpful if your content also goes through a translation or localization process.

Ask your development teams or in-house technical architects about options to get content into your build more efficiently. You could even use the requirements-gathering workshop to outline your team's ideal solution and select something suitable.

Prototype a different way of working

If you feel the content team set-up is preventing content designers from doing more than reactive, surface-level work—perhaps the team functions as a shared service that works across both product design and marketing, or as a centralized design function while product designers are embedded within product teams—it might be time to trial something new.

Sit down with the design or UX lead, explain the limitations of your current structure, and share your proposed approach. If there's no appetite for a structural change, suggest adopting the new approach on a trial basis for a short time; for example, fully embedding a content designer into a product team for an entire project or initiative.

If you do have a centralized team, it can also help to try assigning content designers to a particular area, so they work on similar requests and aren't continually context-switching. This way they can focus on building skills in either product design, optimization work, or marketing content. This suits some people but might not be right for those who thrive on variety.

Testing a new approach can create advocates for change who will help you make the case for longer-term improvements.

Improve pair-writing practices

In *Content Design*, Sarah Winters wrote that pair writing:

> gives you double the brain power. It's like getting through the first and second draft simultaneously. The results are powerful, but the process can be both challenging and productive.

Pair writing between content designers and stakeholders can be done as scheduled one-to-one sessions, but it also works if you offer drop-in availability. Although drop-ins will result in

Purpose
Who is our target audience?
What are the key user needs?
What do we want our user to think, feel or do?

Key messages
What do we need to tell our users (based on our research)?

Voice and tone
What is the brand's voice? What's the relevant tone?

Process
What will our design process be?

Success criteria
How will we measure success?

FIG 4.9: A simple content canvas template can capture the rationale behind the content and serve as a quick reference throughout the design stage.

taking on low-impact (and often invisible) work in the short term, it can also enhance the visibility of content processes and encourage content designers to be more open with their "scrappy" work. At one company, the practice really helped get stakeholders thinking more like content designers and even convinced the legal team to move away from a "print what we tell you" mentality toward a much more collaborative approach.

To make pair writing effective, you need to ensure both parties are aligned on the content goals. They need to agree on the target audience, the user story or job story they're designing for, and the objective of the content. A content canvas is a great way to quickly capture the key information that informs the content, and it can be kept alongside designs as a reference point (**FIG 4.9**).

Pair writers should move into copy creation only once they agree on the key messages—then they can iterate on copy until they have something they're happy with. The content designer can also continue to refine the copy options after the pair-writing session.

Show solid examples

When talking to stakeholders about changing processes and workflows, it can be constructive to look outside your organization to what's happening in other, more mature organizations. Using external examples is often more positive and encouraging than just saying, "We're doing this all wrong," or "We should be working differently." I've found leadership teams are often influenced by success stories about their competitors.

If you have contacts in those companies, ask them for help. Invite them in as guest speakers to an all-hands team meeting to talk about how they're achieving an effective design process or to share how they've embedded content into their product teams. You could even offer to take your leadership team on a field trip to one of those companies to see how they operate.

If you don't have any suitable contacts, seek out talks or presentations from people in organizations you admire and share them internally as inspiration. You don't need to frame it as "We should do this." A simple "I found it really interesting to see how X has overcome similar problems" is a nice introduction.

If you can, find an ally on the design team who's also looking for ways to improve design processes (maybe you have a design ops counterpart). Together, create suggestions for how your teams could work differently, and share your thoughts collaboratively with your leadership team. Show what you'll be trialing and explain when you'll share results.

FIX, THEN FLEX

No one wants to be bogged down with processes and documentation. The idea behind many of these suggested templates is to guide people into better habits and get them moving in the right direction. Once teams are working more fluidly, perhaps they won't need rigid templates or maps. The idea is to fix the blockers, then let teams flex their approach—as long as they don't slip back into inefficient ways of working.

It's tempting to think you need to solve every problem you've identified yourself, but there will be times when you just can't fix it alone. In those cases, you'll need to bring the right people together or convince a sponsor to take on the challenge so you can move on to solving your next problem. To convince them, you'll need robust research, a clear problem statement, and an idea of the expected outcomes that solving the problem will achieve—for example, an estimate of time or efficiency savings. Stay in touch with the sponsor or working group to get regular updates on how the work is progressing. You'll be their link to the content team, so a good working relationship is vital.

If you have one team that adapts well to these new ways of working, use them as an example—your shining beacon of multidisciplinary success! Thriving content designers can use their influence to share knowledge and can even, by establishing standards, start to democratize some of the content work.

5 ESTABLISHING STANDARDS

AS YOUR CONTENT TEAM GROWS, how do you make sure everyone designs in a way that provides consistency and familiarity for customers?

Common standards help achieve design consistency within your content team and beyond, making it easier for teams to make design and content choices. And while it probably won't be the case that teams will automatically follow your guidance perfectly, standards provide clarity when people aren't sure.

Standards aren't about "correcting people's content"—they're meant to improve your users' experience. In Strategic Writing for UX, Podmajersky suggests not positioning the guidance as "rules":

> I get my team to understand that content quality and consistency isn't about robotically following rigid grammar or punctuation rules. It's about making consistent choices—applying content as a tool to help the customer do what they're in the experience to do. [...] If I focus on making the style guide too early, before the team knows what impact the content can make, I end up with some lovely documentation that nobody uses (and everybody resents).

I like to think of standards as the foundational building blocks that help anyone create effective content. Whether you need messaging guides, content models, test or audit templates, or other types of guidance, there are plenty of standards that ops can, and should, play a fundamental role in developing.

Standards are even more effective when integrated into design systems. Whether you already have a design system or your company's just starting to think about creating one, standards should sit within it as integrated guidance. There are many good reasons to integrate design and content, not least because the two disciplines (content and design) will never be used separately.

An operational perspective will help you establish and manage common standards, including identifying what standards you need, how to build them, where should they live, and how to encourage their adoption.

DEFINING STANDARDS

Maybe you do have voice or messaging guidelines tucked away somewhere—but how are they used, and how often? How much documentation is there on adapting tone for UX writing? How consistent are the button and field labels on your website or app?

If you've already spotted issues like this in your discovery work, you might have a good idea of the standards you need. If you haven't, assessing the content and any existing guidelines is a good place to start, and your customer experience map is a good reference point. Design teams might also have their own pet peeves they want to share—perhaps they've seen ten different ways to say "thank you" across the app, and they'd love to get that down to one. Jess Sattell, a senior content designer at Adobe who worked on their design system, told me she suggests starting with data:

> *How many times a month does somebody ask you about how to capitalize something, or what the "right word" is for a specific situation? Tallying the kinds of questions you get asked over a period of three months can bring you lots of insights.*

When defining what you need, consider who will be using the standards and why. If you need to design guidance for non-writers—for example, designers, developers, or subject-matter experts—you'll probably need to consider inclusion of more basic brand voice or writing guidance. If you're designing for seasoned content creators, they might expect to see more detailed rationale for your guidance.

Common standards might include:

- Voice and tone guidelines
- Style guides
- High-level writing guides
- SEO guides
- Accessibility guidelines
- Component patterns
- Messaging matrices
- Content models
- Test templates
- Audit frameworks

Let's look at what goes into some of the most important standards your content team (and beyond) might need.

Messaging matrices

A messaging matrix sets out propositions or product descriptions in a centralized document to ensure consistency across channels. If you work in an organization with a lot of product information, feature names, or technical terms, a matrix will provide a common approach for writing about these things. If your journey-mapping workshop showed that your messaging varies wildly, the matrix will get you back on track.

Assemble your messaging matrix (usually a spreadsheet) through a series of collaborative workshops with your marketing team or subject-matter experts. Choose one type of content or messaging to focus on in each workshop:

1. Begin the workshop by collecting and summarizing all existing versions of the messaging. If you've already mapped out the customer experience, this becomes a little easier.
2. Discuss any specific requirements for the messaging. For example, there might be character limits or space constraints. The messaging might appear alongside other similar messag-

ing on the website. There might be nonnegotiable terms or concepts the subject-matter experts need to communicate.

3. Once everyone has shared their messaging constraints, iterate on the messaging to come up with a version that works for everyone. This is a good opportunity to use pair writing.

4. Bring your options together to see if the group can agree on one version. If not, you might need more than one; for example, you might find you need a shorter snippet and longer version of the same message, depending on where the content will surface. Suggest usability or comprehension testing if there's any uncertainty about how users might perceive the messaging.

Once you're happy with the messaging options, add them to your matrix. Your matrix should include any variations that might have been agreed on. This is particularly useful if your team uses a headless CMS with different content owned by different functions, as you can see how the different versions work together in one place.

Like many standards, your messaging matrix should be a living, evolving document, updated as you learn more about what works best for the users or the business. Decide who owns the matrix and who will make any updates going forward. The group will need to agree to any revisions in the same spirit they were created, so monthly working sessions can be a good way to manage this collaborative effort.

Content models

Content models demonstrate how content types are assembled, how their elements sit together, and how they relate to one another. They're a really useful way to:

- Determine common page structures
- Ensure your content is built correctly in the CMS
- Select content attributes that will affect categorization, taxonomies, or URL structures

HERO	
H1 (Header title) Use this to set the expectation of the page, orient your user, and help Google find your page. The language of the header should reflect your user's search terms and describe what's on the page. It should also be consistent with the link the user has clicked to get to this page.	**IMAGE** This is where your supporting lifestyle image goes. Your image should be 90px × 90px and include alt text which describes the image.
Subheader Use this to draw in the user with a compelling short teaser sentence summarizing why this content is relevant to them.	
PRODUCT INFORMATION	
H2 Title Use this to explain the product you're presenting to the reader.	**PRODUCT IMAGE** This is where your product image goes. Your image should be 60px × 60px and include alt text which describes the image.
Body copy Use this to explain the product benefits. Use bullet points to list out key features.	
Testimonial Use this to showcase a customer testimonial or review, including star ratings.	**CTA** Use this to provide a route for the user to find out more. Keep copy active and concise.

FIG 5.1: A basic content model for a product page helps anyone pulling a product page together know what to include and why.

For example, a content model for a product page shows the content elements used to build the page, and, within those elements, which components can be used and what their attributes are (**FIG 5.1**). The model might also include guidance for each element or outline why that particular one is used over another. Documenting repeatable content structures like this makes content creation more efficient and consistent. It also helps new team members understand how your structures work and gets them up and running much more quickly.

Content models can take many forms, depending on what you want to model and what problems your models will solve. To engage your team with content modeling—which can become quite technical when you start getting into the detail of more granular attributes such as word counts or layout specifications—start broad, with high-level mapping of content types, before zooming in to the detail of the attributes you want to define.

Document your models in the way that's most useful for the audience. For example, if you're defining CMS configuration rules, can you add your guidance directly into the CMS so users don't need to wade through a spreadsheet? Or should your guidelines form part of the onboarding for new content designers so they create consistent content right from the start?

While other standards may be considered general guidance to help with decision-making, content models tend to be more rigid; for example, naming conventions or tagging guidance need to be more tightly followed to enable clear content findability in your CMS or for search engines.

Test templates

It's great when content designers have evaluated a journey and spotted areas ripe for optimization. But they often don't know how to convince their product manager to act on it, or how to articulate their suggestion to marketing colleagues. This is a shame, as small content changes (such as a button or navigation label) can be done relatively cheaply and easily, are quick to implement, and can have a big impact.

Of course, no one wants to negatively impact the performance of a page. A/B tests (where some users see the current version of copy and other users see the test version) are a way to assess the impact of a change before committing to it. It helps to document a consistent way for content designers to propose and record tests. Create a test template (**FIG 5.2**) that includes:

- **Reason to test:** A brief description of what isn't working well in the current experience.
- **Hypothesis:** The impact the content designer thinks the change will have. Try consistent phrasing like "We believe that [change] will [outcome] for [audience]."
- **Proposed test:** An explanation of the content change they want to test.
- **Success measure:** The expected results of the test (usually quantifiable data).

Copy test name	Button label on product description
Reason to test	It says "buy now" which hints at commitment, but the link actually takes you to a further details page
Hypothesis	We believe changing the button label to something less frightening will encourage a higher click-through rate for users
Proposed test	Revise the button copy to "See more"
Success measure	Click-throughs on button increase by 5 percent

FIG 5.2: Test templates are a great way to track progress, keep stakeholders up to date, and give product managers confidence in making changes to page designs.

Audit frameworks

Audits create an inventory of content and enable teams to assess what they have so they can maintain and improve it over time. Auditing content is an important practice that is especially useful for:

- **Assessing content quality:** Creating a content inventory brings the right information together in one place to help analyze specific factors such as accessibility, performance, or brand voice.
- **Identifying areas for optimization:** One mistake content teams often make—not deliberately—is not maintaining their content once it's live. There are always good intentions to go back and iterate or optimize, but somehow content designers just never get around to it. If optimization isn't happening, the team also can't gain insights from making small, tactical changes. An audit can jump-start thinking in this area.
- **Maintaining content:** Regular auditing helps avoid content debt ; when a site continues to grow organically without regular or ongoing audits, content will likely become fragmented, inconsistent, or out of date. At some point, someone has to deal with the sheer volume of all this content.

- **Preparing for a redesign:** An audit is a helpful activity to do before a site or app redesign. It helps the team understand what content they need to keep, merge, get rid of, or revise. They can then work out the right architecture for the content that needs to move—and ditch the rest.

Simple audit tools and guidance make auditing processes much easier.

The audit template

An audit template should allow teams to capture their content-assessment criteria. I've always found a spreadsheet to be the best and easiest format for this template (**FIG 5.3**).

You'll first need to run a site crawl to extract the page data, using a tool like Screaming Frog or OnCrawl. The data can then be cleaned up and dropped into the spreadsheet template. Crawls commonly include data such as:

- Page title
- URL path
- Search title
- Meta description
- Unique page views (if you've included analytics data in the crawl)
- Bounce or exit rates
- Average time on page

Then add columns to your template for qualitative data such as:

- Content type
- User journey stage
- User goal
- Business goal

Your qualitative criteria should be based on the audit's specific purpose. For example, if you're auditing for findability, your template should include columns for criteria such as

Page title	URL path	Search title	Meta description	Unique page views	Av. time on page	Bounce rate	Content type	User journey stage	User goal	Business goal	Findable from Google?	Findable on site?	Accurate?	On brand?
XXXXX	XXXXX	XXXXX	XXXXX	XXXXX	XXXXX	XXXXX	XXXXX	XXXXX	XXXXX	XXXXX				
XXXXX	XXXXX	XXXXX	XXXXX	XXXXX	XXXXX	XXXXX	XXXXX	XXXXX	XXXXX	XXXXX				
XXXXX	XXXXX	XXXXX	XXXXX	XXXXX	XXXXX	XXXXX	XXXXX	XXXXX	XXXXX	XXXXX				

FIG 5.3: This audit template, based on the one in *Content Everywhere* by Sara Wachter-Boettcher, includes columns for different types of page data as well as qualitative assessments.

relevance, commercial value, or usability. For these types of qualitative assessments, you can either use a numbered scoring system or a red-amber-green (RAG) rating: red means the page doesn't meet the criteria, amber means it partially meets the criteria, and green means it does meet the criteria. Some of the content might need further investigation to rate or score it (to rate usability, for example, content designers might need to conduct a heuristic analysis).

It's better to audit a large site in chunks rather than trying to tackle it all at once. You could even designate an afternoon a week as "audit time" to work through the site gradually but consistently.

Audit actions

Include an "Actions" column in your audit template so the team can assign actions based on the assessment. These might be actions like:

- Remove
- Update
- Merge
- Improve
- Move

If possible, assign action owners in the spreadsheet, and include a status column to show the action's progress. I also include a "Priority" column so teams know which actions should be addressed first. Here's how to help team members define their priorities:

- **High-traffic pages:** High-traffic pages that convert well to purchase should be considered high priority, especially if the audit identified issues that are detrimental to the customer experience, such as incorrect information. Teams might want to A/B test any content changes for less critical issues to make sure they don't negatively impact conversion for high-traffic pages.
- **High-risk pages:** Out-of-date information or incorrect legal content should also be high priority, even on pages that don't get much traffic. Just one customer stumbling upon this content could lead to bigger problems.
- **Low-traffic or low-risk pages:** Less-trafficked pages or less-critical issues are lower priority and can be picked up as and when the team can get to them.

A word of caution: some content removal may be obvious, such as pages that are never viewed or out-of-date campaigns. But before removing any pages, the team should check the SEO impact, as well as understand where the content sits. For example, if the content is linked to from multiple sources (either internal or external), they may need to set up redirects. Deletion can feel like a quick task, but shouldn't be done without investigation.

All content should be considered both through a business-value lens and a customer-detriment lens. And if the team identifies any optimization opportunities, make sure they share these with their product managers and get them added to their product backlogs. Refer back to the test template (**FIG 5.2**) to help with this, or carry out deeper heuristic analyses.

CONTENT GUIDANCE FOR DESIGN SYSTEMS

A design system is an established way to collate replicable elements, patterns, tools, and guidelines to make sure anyone designing for a brand does so consistently. They're becoming

Tooltips

Tooltip example

What they do	Point out a new feature and the benefit of using it
How to write them	With the user benefit at front of mind, imagine your 'elevator pitch' for the feature
Do	- Keep them short – no more than 2 lines - Sell the benefit of the feature - Explain how to use or access the feature as succintly as possible

[Here's something new which will help you do x]

Too small? Swipe right to see your image in full screen mode

FIG 5.4: This guidance for tool tips explains what a tool tip does and the formula for writing one alongside an example.

common for visual design, but the vital missing part is often content and how it's used in tandem with the design components.

The ideal design system marries content and design guidance together in the way they will actually be used and experienced. Combining them ensures that design components are based on realistic content and that the content reflects the intention of the design, helping all designers make better decisions.

To illustrate the importance of content in design systems, let me tell you a story. I once worked on a team that discovered a 71 percent conversion improvement by A/B testing the copy on a button element. But when we went to apply the change across the site, we discovered that the button element had been built with a character limit based on unrealistic placeholder copy. Since the content management system was only based on the visual aspect of the design, we were stuck with the constraint and couldn't update the button copy. When non-content creators build content decisions into design systems, you can end up with bad or constrained content at scale.

It's also crucial for content guidance to be contextual to design components (**FIG 5.4**)—it's not enough to just tack your style guide or brand voice guidance onto the end of the design system. In *Expressive Design Systems*, Yesenia Perez-Cruz makes the point that design systems create better products when "all of your brand elements work together as one." A style guide separated from the design context won't be much help when what the system's really crying out for is specific guidance around button labels and help links.

Making the case

Creating a fully comprehensive design system is no easy task—it takes a lot of time, people, and vision. Even if your company has an existing design system team, it might not have a content designer on the team, so you'll need to make the case for content inclusion.

It can take years to build a full-fledged system, so it's okay to start out small and simple. You could begin with basic component guidance, such as button labeling, then scale over time to include more complex patterns, like error messages.

If you already have a design system, you'll need to know what's in it and establish which parts of your content guidance could best sit contextually within the system. Engage your design colleagues early and discuss the importance of integrating content into the system. Share your research and explain which of the existing system components are in most urgent need of guidance to improve the user experience.

I spoke with Amy Thibodeau, who worked on Shopify's Polaris design system. She recommends also stressing the impact design systems can have on changing the way designers approach content:

> *Design systems can influence the way we work together, and by having content separate, we're reinforcing that understanding the way language works isn't a required ingredient. Content isn't a "nice to have." People need to understand how language works at the same level they understand the visual language and front-end code. Build the frameworks that reinforce this.*

If the design system already exists, explain how your frameworks or guidance could work alongside the existing design components and UI guidelines. Once you have this view, it's easier to articulate your vision and discuss feasibility with product designers. Jess Sattell told me that she advises people to visualize their ideas:

> *Create a proposal for what you could add to that page. Just showing the potential for the kind of information that you*

could add is very compelling, since it's enriching what's already there, and likely without major needs for code changes to accommodate it.

Once your teams are invested, work together to create a vision for what you ultimately want to achieve and to determine how to accommodate content guidance alongside the UI components. Discuss the format and structure: Will you need a list of dos and don'ts? Will you include rationale for the guidance (such as research data)? Bringing guidelines to life visually or with examples will make them engaging and easier for people to use.

If you've already gathered the existing content patterns in your journey, share this with the product designers, too. If they're at the early stages of design system work and haven't started collating any patterns yet, they'll find it very useful.

Together you'll also need to determine how to integrate the system with the tools designers are already using. If a working component library is already integrated with design tools, how could your content guidance be built into that? The format or location may also determine whether you'll need to create any onboarding to show users how to use the guidance.

Defining your guidance

If you have an idea of the components most in need of guidance, you'll have to start gathering and assessing them so you can determine what kind of instructions will go into your design system. Select a core group of people from your content team who can meet on a weekly basis and aim to tackle one or two components together at each session.

Start with a single, granular interface component—for example, a Continue button or a Sign In link—and find all the different versions that exist across your whole site or app. Are they always the same, or do wild inconsistencies exist? Capture your findings in one place so you can see all the variations together. As you document what exists, make sure each component has a clear name—for example, "progression buttons" or "field labels."

Once you've identified all your simplest components, move on to increasingly more complex patterns such as error messages or tool tips, then to richer content. Ask questions like:

- Is it in the right tone for the context?
- Does it reflect your brand voice?
- Do we have data or research to show which variation is most effective?
- Do repeated patterns always follow a standard format?
- Are headers and subheaders used correctly?
- Does the content follow accessibility best practices?
- Is the content findable? Does it follow SEO best practices?

Write down any areas that look like they might need more guidance, and compare them to any current frameworks and guidelines that content designers work with (even if they're currently informal guidelines—your design system is about formalizing these). Create a central repository so it's easy to see what you have. What are the gaps in your current guidance? How could existing guidance fit into the current design system? What needs to be changed in the guidance or the system to provide the most value to design teams?

Understanding how much new guidance needs to be created will help you decide whether you need a full-time content designer dedicated to the design system work. If you have a lot to create, trying to chip away at it bit by bit with your team could take a long time.

Creating the guidance

When it comes to defining the details of your guidance, again start with basic patterns and guidelines. For example, you might start with guidance for button components. Buttons are used for multiple situations—including progression (such as going forward or backward), adding items to a cart, submitting information, and confirming or canceling actions—and you'll need guidance for each use case.

Once you've created guidelines for a few basic patterns, you can move on to develop more complex types of guidance,

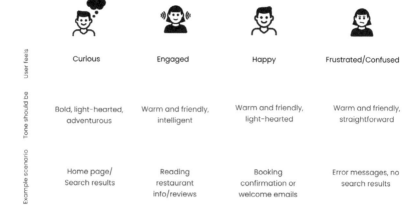

User feels	Curious	Engaged	Happy	Frustrated/Confused
Tone should be	Bold, light-hearted, adventurous	Warm and friendly, intelligent	Warm and friendly, light-hearted	Warm and friendly, straightforward
Example scenario	Home page/ Search results	Reading restaurant info/reviews	Booking confirmation or welcome emails	Error messages, no search results

FIG 5.5: This framework introduces what the component is, what it's used for, and how to write the content, alongside simple dos and don'ts and a visual example.

such as creating standard frameworks for error messages or confirmation messages (**FIG 5.5**). While the design system might already include instructions on how to use a particular component or pattern from a visual design point of view, your specific guidelines should focus on introducing the component, explaining when to use it and how to structure or word it, suggesting what tone to use, and offering helpful language hints or tips. You may also want to include any evidence-based rationale for these decisions.

As your team develops the guidance content, don't forget to stress-test it with non-content designers. A good design system is easy to use and is adaptable to almost every scenario. If a non-writer can easily use the content guidelines and produce the expected output, then you're doing great.

MANAGING STANDARDS

When planning the scope of your standards work, be sure to account for two crucial activities: driving adoption through advocacy, and evolving the standards over time.

You might want to ask how the product designers are (or will be) managing their side of the design system. Can you replicate their model? For example, if they already have a design system working group to manage contributions and feedback, could you add content designers to it? If they don't have one, is this something you could jointly create?

Encouraging adoption

Successful standards speed up the design process and give your design teams more time to solve the bigger problems, so fast adoption is key to achieving impact. But driving adoption takes work. Adobe's Jess Sattell told me it's often harder to advocate for standards than it is to build them in the first place:

Be prepared to constantly remind people about the existence of your standards and where to find them. This is part of the content standards work that a lot of content designers don't consider when they set out to make standards: that there's a lot more work involved in maintaining and bringing awareness to the existence of standards than the work of writing and publishing them.

You'll need careful planning to launch your guidance and make sure the standards are widely used. Be prepared for a launch to take weeks or months—not a day! You might decide to roll out your standards bit by bit rather than all at once. A gradual rollout not only allows an iterative way to build, but also allows you to test and learn how people respond to the guidance. Sattell also stressed the importance of avoiding a big bang:

It's really important for people to know that you're not just creating guidelines and going "ta-da!" and then you're done. It's a culture shift within an organization that requires a long haul of diplomacy, building relationships with partner teams, and consistently reminding and pointing people to resources within the design system documentation when they have questions.

Rather than focusing on the importance of standards for their own sake, demonstrate to people how standards can help make their jobs easier. Torrey Podmajersky told me that's how she helped drive adoption of Google's design system:

> *What's important to people is that their work is successful, and that their customers are successful. I show them how these tools make their work and their customers more successful, and then they self-serve without me.*

Even once people are using your guidance, your work isn't done. In fact, that's often just the beginning. You'll continue your advocacy work long after launch, and you'll need a clear plan for iterating your standards as they're tested and you start getting feedback.

Governing standards

Once your standards are live and adopted, they will need to evolve and grow alongside your team. To ensure the guidance is properly governed over time, you will need to determine the answers to questions like:

- Who will own the content standards? If you're not lucky enough to have a dedicated design system team, who will maintain it?
- Who will help coordinate feedback from working groups?
- Who will be responsible for updating the guidance?
- Who will communicate changes to the wider team?
- How much of someone's time will these tasks take?

If you won't have anyone to maintain and evolve your design system, creating one can cause more problems than it will solve.

When you do make changes or include contributions based on feedback, share the news widely. Yesenia Perez-Cruz told me this helps you get buy-in and encourages people to be part of it: "Emphasize this was a shared win. People will want to be part of the celebration."

A community of practice, working group, or regular forums and workshops are all sensible ways to help gather feedback, test changes, and adapt standards. Set clear expectations for any content designers who want to be involved. Establish a collaborative relationship with users, welcoming their suggestions and working together on solutions. In her conversation with me, Amy Thibodeau said she advises making sure these sessions are safe spaces:

> *Create inclusive rituals that allow people to feel a shared sense of ownership over the design system, where they can discuss it, workshop it, and contribute back. It takes a village to maintain and care for a system that is able to evolve as quickly as software needs to evolve.*

Let collaborative, cross-functional feedback determine what else could be brought into your suite of guidance. Be led by the system's users, and you'll have a truly user-centered system that genuinely helps people create better content.

FOUNDATIONS TO BUILD UPON

Standards provide a base, but that base isn't set in stone. Guidance should be flexible and should evolve as necessary, as you learn from the teams using them. That's why continual feedback and iteration are so important—to help you adapt standards as needed.

With the right foundations now in place for how to build, test, and maintain your content, teams should have a clear blueprint for success. But the launch of any new tool or system is only a starting point, not the end goal. It's the beginning of systemized content creation and maintenance, with the goal of creating a more impactful customer experience.

Having the right guidance, templates, tools, and process is a great start, but better working also depends on communication and cooperation. Connecting people and helping them find ways to collaborate is a key skill for anyone in leadership. In the next chapter, we'll see how an operational approach can help us do exactly that.

6 FOSTERING COLLABORATION

FOR CONTENT DESIGNERS to be effective in their work, they need to build relationships with other teams and work collaboratively all the way through the design process. This collaboration is key for better business outcomes—the resulting experience will be far more connected, relevant, and cohesive.

However, collaboration can be hindered when:

- People are protective about their processes or their content
- People don't understand the value of content design, or assume it's "just the words"
- There's a breakdown in communication within a team or with other teams

Sometimes fostering more collaborative work comes down to educating teams about the role of content, but providing practical help in the way of frameworks and workshops will also help get content designers and their teams and stakeholders working better together. In this chapter, we'll take an operational approach toward fostering effective collaboration across the organization.

WORKING WITH PRODUCT TEAMS

Multidisciplinary product teams leverage individual strengths to become stronger as a whole. But their teamwork depends on each team member relinquishing individual power and embracing shared responsibility. Few teams are able to recognize that the user experience is the result of the contributions of all team members.

Teams also need to recognize the expertise each member brings. If a product designer is creating content and copy, which might not be their strength, it's going to take them longer to get their job done. Having different specialties makes the team more effective, helps team members feel their contributions are valuable, and gives people confidence. Having confidence is essential for a team to be able to push innovative ideas and take considered risks, and it empowers individuals to find their voice and initiate collaboration.

Content designers often have to work hard to find collaborative opportunities where they can demonstrate their value, and to initiate collaboration themselves. I used to tell my team that one of their objectives was to "make a nuisance of themselves"—when they heard a project being discussed that didn't (yet) have content involvement, they needed to speak up and remind the team to include them. But it can be hard for content designers to be proactive when they aren't included early enough in the design process and don't have the time or motivation to muscle in.

When content designers hear about a product meeting they haven't been included in, they can gently nudge meeting organizers to extend an invitation, since often this oversight isn't deliberate. In *Writing Is Designing*, Andy Welfle and Michael Metts suggest three tactics to help content designers get more involved:

1. **The Listen-In:** "Hey, it sounds like you're making some important decisions in that meeting. Can you add me just so I can listen in?" The idea of "just listening in" is a non-threatening way to get into the room.

2. **The Productivity Enabler:** "It seems like that topic relates to what I'm working on now. Could you add me to the meeting? I'd hate for any changes to come late and block the dev team." This reminds product managers that everyone is working toward the same goal.
3. **The Helping Hand:** "I know a workshop activity we could do to get the team aligned. Are you open to me facilitating that for the group?" This creates an opportunity for a collaborative design workshop or ideation session. As a pragmatist, this is the tactic I employ most often; it's led to many design colleagues appreciating how a content-led approach can help their work.

Once you're in those meetings together, remember that it's not always the product designer who has to "hold the pen," and it's not always the content designer who has to "come up with the words." The best collaboration happens when product designers, researchers, and content designers respect one another's opinions and ask one another for help.

Team trust and health

One of the best product managers I worked with understood that to get the team invested in the product strategy and vision, they had to be part of creating it. We collectively created our product vision, and each quarter we would—together—look at our business targets, then explore what opportunities we had to improve the product experience to help achieve those targets. We were trusted to make the right decisions, so as a team we trusted each other and were happy to collaborate.

Operations can help foster this kind of trust by checking in on team health. Health checks come in a number of guises, but most look like a questionnaire with statements about team trust, morale, and mood, which individuals can anonymously rate with a Likert or red-amber-green scale. Your health check should include statements such as:

- We love going to work and have great fun together
- We are a totally gelled superteam with awesome collaboration

- We trust one another
- We help one another deal with problems and resolve issues together
- We understand one another's roles on the team

Low scores on statements about teamwork can indicate challenges in team trust and collaboration. Try speaking to team members individually to ask where they see teamwork challenges and how they think they could improve things.

Building camaraderie

Helping team members get to know one another away from the backlogs, sketches, and pixels is essential. If a product or project team seems to have problems with cohesion, ask your content designer what activities they've done together outside their product work, and see how they respond to the idea of a team activity.

It isn't easy to bring a team together for what may be perceived as "forced fun," particularly for a remote team. Springing "wacky races" or a big, themed party on people can backfire. Anything you do to bring more cohesion to a team has to be inclusive, to help people feel at ease while also learning more about one another:

- Your team may have many different personality types; introverts in particular may balk at the idea of social activity. It isn't that people don't want to socialize, but some may take longer to feel comfortable with coworkers. Creative tasks or fun learning activites, like museum trips or cooking classes, can help take the pressure off.
- Some team members may prefer to keep their personal and work life completely separate. Try to arrange team activities within work hours—some people can't, or don't want to, spend non-work time on a work activity. (I admit I'm one of those people.)
- Some people enjoy the competitive energy of team sports or board games; for others, those activities are their idea of

hell. Try games that encourage team members to work with, rather than against, one another.

- Many people in UX work enjoy artistic activities and opportunities to show off hidden talents. But there should never be any pressure for people to be "good" at something—don't let creative activities become a competition.

Look for activities that can take people away from the day-to-day work without being too polarizing. I once organized a team day outing doing screen-printing; although we were all together, it was a focused, individual activity. One of the content designers on my team was very reserved, to the point that some people thought he was rude. But the screen-printing activity gave him an opportunity to bond with other members of the team in a completely different environment. He was like a different person in the office the next day, and the team was much more eager to collaborate on work.

Helping content designers collaborate

Sometimes team members want to collaborate more, but don't know how to get started or don't have an appreciation of one another's skills. If you can equip your content designers with simple techniques to encourage codesigning—like project frameworks, conversational ideation workshops, and premortems—then they'll have the confidence to initiate collaboration more often and demonstrate their impact.

A project framework

If content designers find themselves brought in too late to projects, left out of research, or deprived of the same context the rest of the team has, a *project framework* can help. Plenty of project canvases exist, but many can be filled in once and then forgotten. The purpose of this framework, on the other hand, is to keep adding to it as the work progresses—you can even capture plans or designs in it. It's an artifact that can be used to help teams get aligned, present their work to others, record decisions, and demonstrate rationale (**FIG 6.1**).

DISCOVERY APPROACH	DESIGN AND BUILD APPROACH	TEST APPROACH	MEASUREMENT APPROACH
What do we already know? How will we find out more?	What constraints or limitations do we have? What activities do we need to do to create something to test?	What will we test? How will we test it?	What will we measure? How will we measure it?
DISCOVERY OUTCOMES What problem are we trying to solve? What are the user needs?		TEST OUTCOMES What did we learn from testing? What will we iterate?	MEASUREMENT OUTCOMES How did it perform?
What are the business needs? What is the opportunity or hypothesis? Which product objectives will this help us achieve?	LEARNINGS FOR FUTURE What did we learn about our product or customers that we can take forward to maximize value in the future?		

FIG 6.1: A project framework is a collaborative way to document the team's work as the project progresses.

A project framework captures:

- **Discovery approach:** What does the team already know, and what does it still need to find out?
- **Discovery outcomes:** What is the problem the team is trying to solve, what do users and the business need, what hypothesis or opportunity does the team have, and what product objectives will the team achieve?
- **Design and build approach:** What constraints or limitations does the team have to work within, and what do they need to create to test their solution?
- **Test approach:** What will the team test and how?
- **Test outcomes:** What did the team learn and what do they need to iterate?
- **Measurement approach:** What will be measured and how?
- **Measurement outcomes:** How did the new design perform?
- **Learnings for the future:** What did the team learn that it could build on in the future?

Identify a physical or virtual space to capture project information. You'll need space to add sticky notes, designs, or notes under each of the questions posed. Any team member can initiate the framework. As the project work progresses, the team should set aside follow-up time to regroup and document progress. These sessions can serve as a checkpoint at the end of each stage of the design and build process.

Most of the work captured in the project framework should be derived from other team sessions; however, bringing it all into one place relies on the team to collaborate and share their knowledge from these other sessions, which is helpful for content designers who might be spread across multiple product teams but still need the same context as everyone else.

Conversational ideation workshop

When the team knows what they're designing for but haven't yet moved into sketching solutions, a *conversational ideation workshop* is a perfect next step. It's a content-first approach to design that gets designers thinking about specific interactions, nudges people away from sketching out empty boxes, and identifies any particular messages or language to include in the user journey.

In this workshop, the team role-plays the conversation the user and business need to have for both parties to achieve the desired outcome. It helps determine a logical order of information, identifies any mismatches between business and user goals, and highlights unexpected user needs that the team will need to design for.

In *Strategic Writing for UX*, Torrey Podmajersky recommended a version of this workshop, which I have tried a few times to great effect. Here's how it works:

1. The team starts by summarizing the user goal and business goal for the journey being designed (**FIG 6.2**). Pin the goals to opposite ends of a wall or virtual space.
2. Divide the team into pairs to role play the journey. In this case, the journey is the conversation that needs to happen for both the user and the business to achieve their goal.

User goal	Business goal
Buy plane ticket	Sell plane ticket

FIG 6.2: The user goal and business goal are posted at opposite ends, with space for the journey between them.

3. In each pair, one person plays the business and the other plays the user. Their task is to have a natural conversation as if there were no digital interface, a bit like a call center conversation. As the two talk, they should write each statement on a card or sticky note (**FIG 6.3**).

4. After they reach their goals, they should summarize their conversation by listing each topic they covered on a new card or sticky note. The topics should then be plotted between the user goal and business goal in the order they talked about them (**FIG 6.4**). They can also look back through their conversation to make sure it's in a logical order and highlight any particular words or phrases they liked, or anything that jumps out as a necessary UI element, like a date-picker.

5. Ask each person to sketch solutions based on their summary. Use rapid sketching to make sure teams generate simple ideas rather than detailed ones—this is just to articulate their first thoughts of how their conversation could translate to an interface. After sketching, ask everyone to share their sketches with the wider group. You might also want to dot-vote the elements of each idea that worked particularly well.

The resulting ideas can then be taken away by the product designer and content designer to further develop into a solution (**FIG 6.5**).

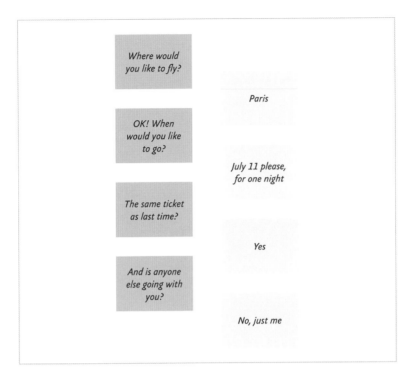

FIG 6.3: Each statement in the role-played conversation is documented on sticky notes.

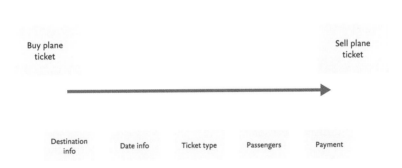

FIG 6.4: Designers summarize the conversation flow as steps in the journey between the user goal and business goal.

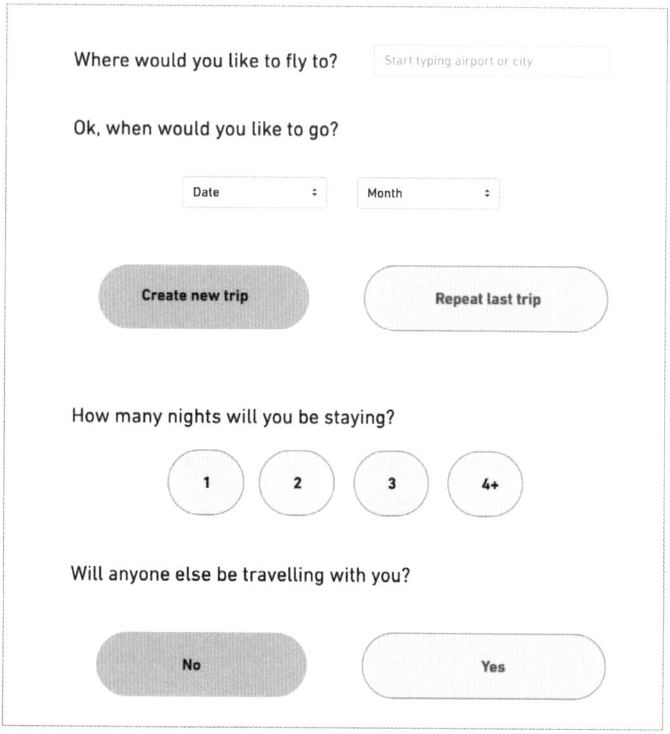

FIG 6.5: Sketches from the conversation ideation workshop can later be turned into a wireframe.

Premortems

A *premortem* is a workshop activity that can be used at the start of a new project or initiative to find out what concerns people, uncover risks to the success of the project, and discuss how to mitigate disaster.

Not only can content designers raise concerns about not being involved at the right times, but they can also hear what product designers or researchers might be worried about. When the team members understand one another's concerns, they can better identify ways to alleviate them ahead of time.

For the premortem activity, the team projects itself into the future, and thinks about all the things that could have gone wrong and why. All a team needs for this is some physical or virtual wall space, sticky notes, and about forty-five minutes:

1. The team starts by imagining everything on the project that has gone wrong in six or twelve months' time. They spend five minutes brainstorming on sticky notes all the things they can think of that went wrong. For example, "The designs weren't suitable for the required content."
2. For the next five minutes, using a different-color sticky note, everyone adds reasons *why* those things went wrong. For example, "Designers made decisions before they knew what the content was."
3. As a team, review what's on the wall and group the sticky notes into any similar themes. Putting your themes into categories like "people," "processes," and "systems" can help you identify the biggest potential risk areas.
4. In the second half of the session, the team reads through the issues identified and spends five to ten minutes thinking up ways to mitigate the bad outcomes. For example, one way to mitigate the problem of designs not being suitable for the content might be: "Provide content before designers start work."

At the end of the final step, the team will understand the biggest areas of concern and the actions they could take to prevent them from becoming a reality. They should capture these in a spreadsheet and assign owners to the actions.

Before wrapping up the session, the team should agree when they will revisit the list of actions to make sure they're giving themselves the best chance of success.

WORKING WITH DEVELOPMENT TEAMS

Ideally, content and development teams work harmoniously and collaboratively at all times. But the nature of our work means that's not always possible, especially when development sits outside of product teams. Different team structures, motivations, and approaches can often lead to communication issues or conflicting views on how things should work. To mitigate these challenges, the content team needs to get development involved early so they can give feedback on the technical feasibility of any solutions, and they should continue to work together throughout the design process.

Sharing and learning is a great way to open up two-way communication. Content designers can gain knowledge of backend systems, and in return share their approach to the user experience and what they hope to achieve. Here are a few small ways to increase communication between content design and development.

Ask more questions

Developers and content designers may not always use the same terminology, but we can take steps to make sure everyone is better equipped to have the right conversations. Some teams have a technical architect or business analyst who can help explain functionality or pull technical requirements together. But often we're at the mercy of our own collaboration, so we need to make sure we can communicate effectively and ask questions when we don't understand.

To write, create, and manage many types of content, content designers need a basic understanding of how the customer journey works behind the scenes. For example, to make sure error messages are clear and provide an effective resolution, designers need to know what triggered the error and how it can be corrected. When asked to create an error message, content designers should ask developers questions like:

- What scenarios could trigger the error?
- Why does the system throw an error like this?
- How could the error be prevented?

Asking these questions will help designers better understand the system. They might even discover a way to prevent the error in the first place—a key principle of interaction design.

Share your goals

Content designers also need to be ready to share with development teams how content is impacted by technical constraints. Sometimes constraints can be removed, but only if the developers fully understand the implications for the end user. Sometimes they haven't even been told it's a problem; content designers should be proactive about having these conversations.

There are also occasions when backend data pulls through to the front end (for example, dropdown entries in form fields), so what may seem like data to developers is also user-facing copy. In these cases, content designers really need to help developers understand the importance of user-centered content and help them come up with solutions for translating and displaying data on the front end.

Don't forget your development teams when you present your design principles or content team vision; this gives them a clear understanding of what you're working toward. It's then much easier to explain how and why something isn't quite right when it doesn't align with the team's vision.

Show, don't tell

Let's say a customer journey is riddled with unclear error messages, jargon, and nonsensical system-generated content. One way to explain why these elements need to be improved is by demonstrating what *good* looks like. Instead of just saying "I'm rewriting this message," prompt content designers to share improved versions of copy with developers. This helps illustrate the difference between what's there presently and the hoped-for solution.

Developers should have as much exposure to user behavior as the rest of the team. Make sure they're invited along to observe usability testing to see firsthand how content, design, and build affect the user experience, and how important it is to get them right. The design team may be aware of something that causes a huge pain point for users, but if developers have never observed users, they may be unaware of just how bad the issue is.

Make sure teams invite developers to research playback sessions, too, or even to provide input on the research definition—maybe developers also want to learn more about users and how they interact with the journey.

Involving the development team helps them become more curious about user experience problems and helps them think more proactively about how backend processes impact them. When developers can see where they can have an impact right from the start, it makes gathering technical requirements easier and encourages more collaborative solutions.

Get comfortable with code

When content doesn't sit within a CMS, content designers may be dependent on developers to make code changes when they need to publish new content or revise existing content. The resulting bottlenecks can be frustrating, especially when the change is small—a typo, for example—and not a high priority for the dev team.

If content and development have a good working relationship, but content designers feel like their needs aren't prioritized, see if it's feasible for content designers to get access to the codebase to make small updates themselves. Developers might be able to spend time training content designers in Github so they're confident the right skills are in place. Empowering content designers to work with the code directly removes frustration and alleviates some of the workload on developers.

STAKEHOLDER MANAGEMENT

Content is often under the scrutiny of many teams, including legal, marketing, product, and customer experience. We need to foster good working relationships so we can find solutions that are right not only for users but also for the business. We may even need to build trust if the content team is newly established and taking over content responsibilities from existing stakeholders.

Luckily, there are a few ways to make stakeholder relations more positive while gaining advocacy for content.

Stakeholder mapping

At the start of any project, when establishing a team—or at any time, in fact—it's a good idea to map your stakeholders. This activity helps you identify those who might need to be kept close, or those you might need to invest extra time in to gain their trust.

Stakeholder mapping can be done as a product team, or the content team might decide to take this on to determine who their content allies could be. Either way, you'll need a wall space (or virtual space), sticky notes, and about an hour of people's time:

1. Create a simple matrix with four boxes (FIG 6.6). Label your vertical axis as "Influence" and your horizontal axis as "Interest."
2. As a group, discuss which of your stakeholders has the most influence in the organization and who has the most and least interest in your work.
3. Once you've identified where they fall in your matrix, discuss how you might communicate with the different groups:
4. Stakeholders with high project interest and high influence should be managed closely.
5. Stakeholders with high interest but low influence should be kept informed.
6. Stakeholders with low interest but high influence should be kept satisfied.
7. Stakeholders with low interest and low influence should be monitored.
8. Once you've captured your ideas, think about communication formats and frequency. This will depend on the type of communication; for example, an email roundup might be weekly, while workshop invitations might be more ad hoc. Ideally, you don't want to end up with lots of different communications for different stakeholders, so focus on the activities that can cover as many of your groups as possible. You might end up with more tailored communications for those you need to manage more closely.

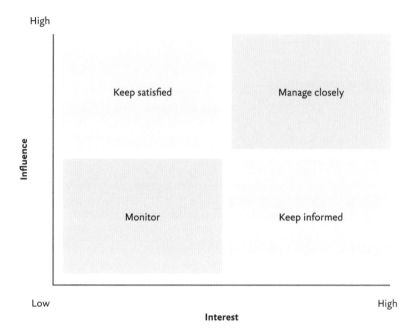

High

Influence

Keep satisfied

Manage closely

Monitor

Keep informed

Low

High

Interest

FIG 6.6: A quadrant map helps you understand which stakeholders you'll need to invest the most time and effort in.

9. At the end of the session, don't forget to assign actions to people to make sure the ideas are followed through on.

This artifact is a useful reference point for planning review meetings and project checkpoints. The team can use it to understand which stakeholders need to be involved, what they might be interested in, who will have the most sway, and who might have more challenging questions.

Involving stakeholders in research

A great way to help stakeholders feel like part of the team is to invite them to observe any usability testing. This is an excellent way for content designers to demonstrate the effectiveness of content, too, particularly to stakeholders who have doubts about content design. If there has been any tension between content designers and stakeholders over the suggested copy, watching users interact with the content can help resolve it.

A few years ago, I challenged some stakeholders on the wording of a question on an insurance form. The question wasn't clear, but, frustratingly, the stakeholders insisted I couldn't change it. I invited them to observe some lab testing, and they saw for themselves that every user struggled to understand the wording—and they agreed to change it. I changed the wording immediately for the remaining testing sessions so the stakeholders could see the improvement and feel comfortable with the change.

When inviting stakeholders to observe test sessions, here are a few tips:

- Set expectations. Remind them of the difference between quantitative and qualitative testing beforehand. This kind of testing won't provide them with quantified data.
- Make sure they can attend for the whole day to see observations in context. A single test won't necessarily demonstrate typical results, and you want stakeholders to have a representative view of the testing.
- Emphasize that their role is to observe and take notes. There's nothing worse than a stakeholder who attends a test session but spends it on calls or checking email, ignoring what's happening in the room.
- Before the session starts, explain the difference between an observation and a solution, so they're not just noting their desired solution. I've been at enough usability test sessions to realize not everyone knows how to capture observations correctly. An observation is something witnessed during testing, such as: "User doesn't see the help link and asks if there is a help link." Rather than writing down the observation, some stakeholders will jump to a solution, like, "Need to make the help link more obvious." Coach them to write down only what happens, not what changes need to be implemented to the design.

After the session, collect all the notes so they can be reviewed, filtered, grouped, themed, and prioritized before anyone comes up with any new solutions. Promise to keep the stakeholders in the loop, but don't promise any immediate solutions.

Presenting to stakeholders

Presentations enhance the visibility of a team's work to other teams and stakeholders. Team presentations take place for a number of reasons:

- To share early explorations of design work to gather support or feedback
- To update stakeholders on progress at predetermined checkpoints
- To gain sponsorship or funding for a project
- To share final designs or project learnings

However, teams often fail to consider the audience and intended meeting outcomes, or don't plan and present collaboratively. When this happens, they don't provide clear context and rationale for the work, fail to answer difficult questions, and leave with their confidence shaken. This can deter content designers from presenting at these sessions and can undermine stakeholder support in your projects.

Your role is to equip teams with everything they need to collaboratively make these sessions effective. For sessions to really showcase team effort and show the rigor behind the work, the team has to be well prepared. This means they:

- understand the purpose of the session and what the outcome should be,
- know the audience and what motivates them,
- know who's presenting what,
- have considered any potential questions and have answers ready, and
- know what's needed from the audience.

Donna Spencer, author of *Presenting Design Work*, recommends that teams start with the end result before showing any process detail. She also recommends they use plain language and avoid throwing around technical terms to discuss the design or features, focusing instead on what the experience will be like for users.

To demonstrate effective teamwork, the whole team should present. This gives content designers the opportunity to talk about areas of the experience that play to their skills, such as particular language or interaction choices. Providing such rationale is a really important way to communicate the rigor of content design. Help content designers feel more confident presenting at these sessions by providing them with a clear and repeatable structure they can use to introduce their content, such as a content canvas or project framework.

It's also great to get teams used to sharing early work in stakeholder presentations, instead of waiting until they have something more polished. This provides transparency and helps give stakeholders a better understanding of the design process and the role each team member plays throughout.

Once the work has been presented, the team should be prepared to answer any questions. To help content designers feel confident about answering questions, they'll need to have been as involved and invested in the work as the product designers. The whole team should know the rationale for any design decisions and be able to preempt any potential questions, as well as explain where they are in the design process and outline next steps.

The team should nominate someone (and rotate the role) to take notes during presentations, so they can reflect on any feedback and questions together after the session. If they need something from the audience, such as feedback or support, they should make this clear at the start of the session.

Rather than repeating sessions for stakeholders who can't attend, encourage teams to record the sessions and share the recordings. If they're dependent on feedback from stakeholders to continue their work, they'll need to provide a clear deadline for any questions or feedback.

Content item	Feedback category	Feedback provider	Comments	Status	
Homepage header		Toni Clare, legal team	The word 'must' isn't quite correct, too strong	Feedback provided	
	Typo/grammar				
	Inaccurate				
	Off-brand				
	Legal issue				
	Usability issue				
	Inconsistent with marketing				

FIG 6.7: A feedback spreadsheet enables you to track not only the feedback itself, but its category and status as well.

Managing stakeholder feedback

I once worked on a project that was overwhelmed with feedback from multiple stakeholders. Some of the feedback was conflicting, much of it was subjective, and it was difficult to keep track of it all. I needed a constructive way to avoid *content design by committee*. I found that the simplest way to capture and manage the feedback was with a spreadsheet (**FIG 6.7**). It's not elegant, but it allows content designers to record the content item, create categories for feedback, capture who the feedback came from, and the specific comments. A final column for tracking the status of the feedback turns the spreadsheet into a to-do list.

Categorizing the feedback helps manage expectations: if a stakeholder's feedback doesn't fit into a category (i.e., it's a subjective opinion), the content designer can politely say thank you, but doesn't need to act on it. Whether a content designer is facilitating a feedback session or gathering feedback via email, they should outline the categories up front. I suggest the following categories:

- **Typo/grammar:** Grammatical or spelling errors and typos
- **Inaccurate:** Factually inaccurate (e.g., wrong pricing or date)
- **Off-brand:** Language the brand doesn't use
- **Legal issue:** Legal or compliance implications
- **Usability issue:** Detrimental to customer experience (e.g., confusing wording on a button label)

- **Inconsistent messaging:** Language not consistent with other customer-facing materials (e.g., wording on the website differs from customer emails)

Once all feedback is captured, the content designer may choose to add a column of alternative copy options and recirculate the whole sheet to stakeholders. It's important for the content designer to avoid rewriting any copy during the feedback session. Good work can't be done on the fly, and there's some risk of a free-for-all as everyone starts suggesting their version. The content designer should take the feedback away, reflect, and then respond, making sure to set clear expectations about how long any revisions might take.

Some tools (such as Gather Content) capture feedback within your workflow, eliminating the need for workshops and separate sessions. But if content designers are running feedback sessions or working with groups of stakeholders, spreadsheets are simple to use and access, and make the feedback visible to all. They can also easily be attached to task tickets in project-tracking software.

LET YOUR CONFIDENT COLLABORATORS SHINE

When all disciplines are working comfortably together and content designers are confidently initiating working sessions and gathering feedback, product teams should see both a real change in the quality of their work and more effective input from content designers. Opening up working practices fosters trust, transparency, and vulnerability, and teaches teams to learn from one another. Once these ways of working extend more broadly into the business—with stakeholders and cross-functional teams communicating early, frequently, and collaboratively—customer experiences will begin to improve, too.

With your content designers making good progress within design teams, it's time for them to help you grow your craft, build advocacy, and further your content contribution to the wider organization.

BEYOND THE TEAM

NOW THAT YOUR TEAM is running effectively, it's time to think about how you can broaden its influence. Outreach will help organizations understand what good content design is and how it can help them across every part of their business.

Sarah Winters told me that one of the biggest barriers to content design adoption in organizations is having it recognized as a skill:

> A lot of organizations are still running on a premise that to produce good content, you just need to think up some words. It's simply not the case. We usually find people simply don't understand the level of skill, time, and effort that needs to go into a piece of really good content design. Once we work in the open and share those skills, views change.

By building and developing our practices, sharing them with the larger community, and demonstrating our impact, we strengthen not only our content team, but also the content design discipline as a whole.

CREATING A COMMUNITY OF PRACTICE

As any team grows, it collectively gains more knowledge and experience. But with embedded or distributed content teams, content designers may not have much to do with one another on a daily basis. To maintain a close-knit content community that can evolve and improve the discipline, you need to work hard to create cohesion.

A *community of practice* brings together people with a shared interest so they can learn and grow in a safe space. Bringing content team members together regularly enables them to:

- Rally around the vision and principles for content as a craft
- Benefit from peer reviews and critiques (crits)
- Share knowledge and learn from one another
- Discuss common themes or topics that impact their work
- Contribute to shared guidelines or frameworks
- Identify opportunities for collaboration
- Bond socially and have fun
- Hold retrospectives and create or review future plans
- Identify initiatives to take on, above and beyond their product work

A strong community of practice also encourages passion for content design, and, in turn, builds advocates who want to go out into the wider business (or even outside the business) to educate others on the value of content.

Getting the community started

Emily Webber, author of *Building Successful Communities of Practice*, recommends starting by clarifying whom the community is for. The community doesn't necessarily need to be just your core content team; you might decide to open it up to anyone in your organization who creates content. This also helps build trust and gain advocacy with other teams. Even if other content creators only pop into community events occasionally, knowing they're welcome is a great first step in building closer relationships.

Once you've determined your core community members, spend time with them to define the community's purpose. A great way to get started is to host a kickoff session. Ask the members to note all the things they'd like to get out of the community and why. Group the ideas and see what themes emerge, then find out how often the team wants to get together to work on the themes. For example, one theme might be peer reviews and critiques, which should happen fairly regularly. Another might be about having fun, so perhaps a monthly social activity or quarterly meetup would be appropriate.

One of the most important things your community should provide is a safe, inclusive space. Candi Williams, head of content design at Bumble, told me:

> *If people don't feel safe, if they feel overwhelmed or undervalued, they're not empowered to do their best work. Good people, a clear and meaningful purpose, and psychological safety are the crucial ingredients for a thriving content design community.*

A supportive community can help content designers gain confidence and find their voice. It's particularly important to ensure that community is safe for people with marginalized identities. It's the job of everyone within the community to elevate one another.

Take time to create a mission statement or community principles, or a manifesto that ties the mission and values together with an emotive element, using the exercise outlined in Chapter 3. These activities help you clarify what is and isn't in scope for the community and to communicate your aims. You should also create a code of conduct for the community so members know what's expected of them and feel confident that it's a safe space.

Conducting critiques

Many content leaders struggle with critique attendance and encouraging people to share their work. It only takes one bad experience for someone to avoid these sessions. In *Content Design*, Sarah Winters says:

Crits can be hard to deal with. It's not easy to let other people tear your work to shreds. It's not easy to listen to them telling you what's wrong with it. Many people naturally fear it turning into a slanging match. That's why crits have rules, so that they become safe environments for meaningful feedback.

I've often thought it unfortunate that *crit* is also short for *critical*. And although crits shouldn't allow people to tear their colleagues' work to shreds, unless teams have been trained to give and receive feedback effectively, that can end up happening.

Crits work best when people put aside egos and focus on solving the problem in a collaborative manner. It can take a while to get content designers comfortable with sharing their early, scrappy work—it demands a level of vulnerability—but once they do, they'll be more open to feedback from other content designers, product designers, and stakeholders. One content designer recently told me she dreaded going into crits, but always came out of them with so much good feedback that she was glad she had done it.

A community crit should feel free from judgment. In *Resilient Management*, Lara Hogan makes the point that "sometimes catching a whiff of incoming critical feedback can threaten any one of our core needs at work." We don't want content designers to feel like their progress is under scrutiny or they're being personally judged. A crit is about building upon what has been started in order to improve upon it, and to make sure the work benefits from different perspectives.

If you identified that crit attendance needs improvement, survey people to find out why they aren't attending. There may be one or two people who haven't been politely constructive in crit sessions and have put others off attending, or some people might not feel they have much to share.

It can also be valuable to open your content community crit sessions up to design and research colleagues, or to host combined product and content design crits. Other disciplines can bring illuminating perspectives and tend not to overanalyze the content as much as content designers might. Just make sure the group doesn't get too big; more than twelve people can be intimidating.

Getting feedback

When content designers are nervous about having their work critiqued, I remind them that it's much easier to critique someone else's work than it is to create the work in the first place—so they've already done the hard bit. It's also helpful to establish a few ground rules so people presenting their work know what to expect and how to receive feedback:

- Share early and often; there's no such thing as too scrappy.
- Dedicate enough time to share work. Formal crits are ideal, as you'll get much better feedback in a formal group session than in a five-minute chat with one other person.
- Provide background context: user needs, business goals, the problems being solved, key messages, and what you want the user to think, feel, or do. Explain how far along in the process you are, too, and any constraints you're working with.
- Be clear about the feedback you want. Are you looking for help with something in particular? Do you need a fresh pair of eyes to see whether something makes sense? Are you hoping to cut down the copy further?
- Stay open to suggestions, challenges, and questions. None of the feedback you'll get is personal; it's about making the user experience even better.
- Document feedback without trying to digest it in the moment. You don't have to respond immediately, and you don't have to act on all feedback. Take time later to reflect on the comments and challenges before revising anything.
- Avoid being defensive if you disagree with feedback or it hasn't been framed constructively. Instead, ask questions to get more context on the person's perspective.
- If you're not sure what someone means, ask them to clarify or provide an example.
- Thank people for their time and input, and, if needed, set a time for a follow-up session to share your progress.

Giving feedback

These sessions are just as important for those giving feedback as those receiving it, because they'll learn how to be constructive and objective in a safe space. Giving feedback is a hard skill to learn, and providing feedback that's specific, actionable, and communicated appropriately takes practice. The more content designers get used to it, the more value they can add to team-work. For those giving feedback:

- Listen attentively and let the presenter finish before providing feedback.
- Take time to reflect and think about the work and how best to articulate your feedback before responding.
- Rushing in with opinions isn't constructive. What *is* constructive is helping the presenter think further about the consequences or impact of any specific decision they've made. Avoid comments such as "I don't like..."
- Try framing your feedback as a question: "Have you thought about...?" or "Did you consider...?" The presenter may have a solid rationale for their decisions.
- Provide positive feedback, too. The aim of the session is to build upon work already started, so if something is great, say so!
- "What if..." or "You could also..." suggestions add more value to the work.
- If you've spotted something you could help with, or that overlaps with work your team is doing, say so.
- Use specific examples to bring your suggestions to life and help clarify what you mean.
- Respect any expectations set by presenters. They will want to take all feedback away to consider before sharing their work again.

You might need to facilitate the first few sessions to get the crits running smoothly, but try to identify a named facilitator for sessions going forward so all content designers get a chance to run them. This will boost their confidence.

Building facilitation skills

Holding a room isn't a skill that comes naturally to a lot of people. But within your content community, you can build in plenty of chances to help content designers learn to present, facilitate, and amplify their work.

In *Presenting Design Work*, Donna Spencer reflects on why presenting can be so stressful:

> *I think the stress has two sources. The first comes from the general difficulty of presenting; the second involves a real lack of clarity about why we present in the first place.*

When people aren't sure what attendees expect from a session, they feel vulnerable and underprepared. We covered tips to help teams prepare for presenting in Chapter 6, but there's more we can do to improve facilitation and public speaking skills.

To help designers overcome the general difficulty of public speaking, create time at each community meetup for short presentations. Start small by offering lightning talk slots or pechakucha-style slots (https://bkaprt.com/lcd41/07-01/). Pechakucha is a fast-paced activity where you can show up to twenty slides for twenty seconds each. These "quick talks" can be based on any topic (you might choose a fun, non-work-related theme). Some people prefer to be assigned a topic for these sessions; you could pick anything from "what you learned last month" to "how your career led to your current role." These sessions are also a great way to help community members become acquainted.

Another route to building facilitation skills is to add a regular mini-workshop slot to your meetups on topics like empathy mapping, ideation skills, or conversational design. Ask content designers to facilitate in pairs as a gentle introduction to facilitation. These sessions also teach community members new methodologies they can take back to their product teams.

Try to create opportunities for everyone to learn facilitation skills. It's often the same people who are keen to take on speaking or facilitation roles in community sessions. While it's great to have people who are willing to do this, a community should allow all content designers to get what they need to from it and become comfortable with speaking or running workshops for their product team.

Make sure content designers know these sessions are a safe space for them to make mistakes; they should feel comfortable asking for feedback. Once team members start feeling more confident, you can suggest they take on wider team lunch-and-learn sessions, or even host the meetups themselves.

Creating a self-managing community

Once your community is up and running, you'll want to step back from the organization to empower team members and give them opportunities to step up, develop, and lead.

From the outset, encourage community members to take ownership of the things they want to get out of it. When content designers become more active in the community, it helps drive engagement at a peer level, rather than always being a top-down mandate.

Stay on hand for support, and join events every few months to ensure the community is still getting what they want from them and that they haven't strayed too far from the community's goals. It's also worth encouraging retrospectives or feedback sessions twice a year, so that team members can celebrate successes and suggest improvements.

Of course, helping your content creators gel is just the start—be prepared for the community to raise further issues for your ops backlog. When teams feel they can talk openly, you'll hear about more pain points in their tooling and workflows. So listen carefully, and respond accordingly.

CREATING LASTING IMPACT

Imagine your content designers becoming known as consultants people seek out for advice—not just for content problems, but for any kind of problem-solving. When content designers can show the rigor of their work, they're more likely to influence product and business strategy. Being proactive about setting success metrics and analyzing data turns content designers into product experts, able to define and solve problems across the business.

To make sure your content designers make an impact across your whole organization, you need to demonstrate success, then show other teams how content can help them achieve the same success.

Define measurable goals

To set good targets up front, content designers need to identify the problem they're trying to solve, and understand how they'll know when they've solved that problem. Unfortunately, several obstacles can get in their way:

- Content designers don't always have access to data or analytics, making it much harder (but not impossible) to measure effectiveness.
- When content designers *do* have access to data, they often only focus on the quantitative measures. Data tells us *what* users are doing, but not *why* they're doing it—so they need to combine quantitative data with qualitative insights.
- Content designers try to track content directly back to company goals or targets. These are often too big and intangible—no one would be able to prove that their content directly increased market share or profitability. Even if we reduce the altitude and look at success indicators or business objectives, these are affected by other factors (like seasonality, pricing, or marketing activity) and aren't in the direct control of the product or service team. We need more granular product objectives.

A clear, repeatable framework will help content designers make sense of the relationship between company goals and product objectives. Everyone doing design work should know the objectives that their work contributes to—it's why they're doing the work.

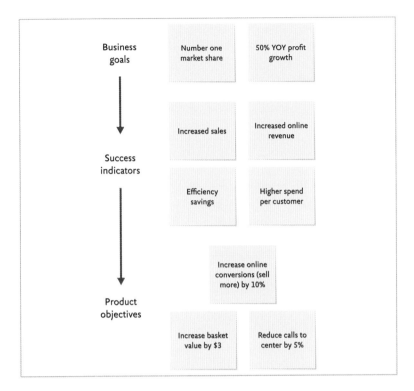

FIG 7.1: Content can't be directly tied to business goals, but it *can* directly impact the product objectives.

Thinking about goals from a top-down approach is helpful (**FIG 7.1**). Whether your company uses goals and KPIs, or objectives and key results, every organization has big, overarching goals to achieve. Below the goals are success metrics which measure movement towards the goals. Contributing to these are the more granular things a product team can influence, like increasing conversions on certain pages or reducing incoming support calls. The product team should identify what they can influence, then set their own measurable objectives with clear, achievable targets.

Understanding how business goals, success indicators, and product objectives connect helps content designers think more strategically about the content they should focus on and what role their content plays in the larger business ecosystem.

If, for example, the product objective is to "increase conversion by 10 percent," there are many content elements that might impact conversion, such as product descriptions, button label wording, and proposition wording. These are all things that content designers can directly control.

Give content designers the best chance of success by making sure they know their product team's objectives and measurements, any overarching content team objectives, and how these all filter down into their own individual objectives. If they don't know their objectives, they can't demonstrate value or help influence product strategy.

When content creators sit on a centralized team, understanding objectives may be trickier. When working on product work, they're contributing to the product objectives, but when working on broader work like marketing content, the objectives are determined by the strategy for that particular piece of work. In this case, the content designer might need to be more proactive about defining their own success metrics.

A handy cheat sheet is a simple way to help content designers see which elements of content they could focus on, according to what the work is trying to achieve (**FIG 7.2**). The cheat sheet will help them decide which content elements they could test, improve, and measure based on the product objectives. For example, if the brand team wants to improve conversion from product page to purchase, the content designer might suggest testing product descriptions or call-to-action labels. Changes could be measured through quantitative data such as click-throughs or sales, or through qualitative data such as an on-page customer feedback survey.

By including a combination of both objective (quantitative) and subjective (qualitative) measurements when defining success, we get better insights. Whether teams use sentiment analysis, user feedback, or anecdotal insights from other areas of the business, qualitative data should not be overlooked. It's as helpful to know what users think and feel about their experience as it is to know whether they did what we intended.

Teach other teams

While you don't want to create extra work for an underresourced team, it's worth investing time and effort in winning advocates and sponsorship for your team's work. Gain stakeholders' trust, and you'll gain more respect for content design.

It takes a lot of work to make your team known, and, depending on what your team wants to be known for, it can take a while to establish your reputation. Think of your outreach as a marathon, not a sprint—a little work over a sustained period has more impact than an intense burst that quickly fizzes out.

Introduce content design

First, make a habit of introducing new team members to everyone and sharing an overview of the kind of work they'll be doing. If possible, do this on Workplace, Slack, or your company social channels.

Once people know who your team is, you can educate them a little more on the role of content. I've found one-pagers useful for explaining content design to the product team and the wider teams they work with (and how to get the best from content designers). The one-pager doesn't need to be a printed document; it could just be an onscreen visual. It might say something like:

> *Content designers:*
> - *work alongside product designers to define the user experience;*
> - *define the best way to communicate key messages based on user needs, paying particular attention to structure, voice, and tone;*
> - *are great facilitators, writers, and problem-solvers; and*
> - *use techniques such as journey mapping and empathy mapping.*
>
> *Get the best from content designers by:*
> - *engaging them early,*
> - *using their research skills,*
> - *designing with them, and*
> - *seeking their input and feedback.*

BUSINESS GOAL	QUALITATIVE MEASURES	QUANTITATIVE MEASURES
Drive awareness or visibility of content	Call center queries/ complaints Social sentiment Survey comments	Page views Click-through rates Site traffic Social shares Call volumes Live chat stats Tree tests
Engagement with content	Sentiment Usability testing Concept testing	Dwell times Likes or shares Page bounce and exit rates Click-through rates Form completion Data submission Comment submission
Comprehension	Usability testing Highlighter testing	Call volumes Live chat stats On-page feedback submissions Click-through rates Dwell times Exit rates Brand sentiment scores
Conversion	Task completion Usability testing Customer feedback	Click-through rates Quotes, sales, or leads Newsletter signups Onboarding completions Page progression
Task completion	Task completion Usability testing Customer feedback	Sales Time to task Onboarding completions Page progression Exit rates

RELEVANT CONTENT ELEMENTS

Navigation
Headers
Meta descriptions
CTAs
Internal links
Categorization of help content
Contextual help
Social sharing links
Notifications or emails

Product /pricing information
Help content
T&Cs or legal information
Forms
Articles
Proposition messaging
Videos
Social media posts
Customer emails
Push notifications

Product/pricing information
Help content
T&Cs or legal information
Form wording
Offer wording
Service emails

CTA labels
Product descriptions
Pricing information
Help copy
T&C wording
Proposition messaging

Self-service journeys
Purchase or renewal journey
Onboarding screens
CTA labels

FIG 7.2: A quick-reference guide to the content that can impact different product objectives is a good way to get content designers thinking more about where their focus should be.

Make the most of any company-wide communication platforms such as Workplace by creating a content team page or wiki. This also helps people put names to the faces on your team and creates an approachable impression. When you share great work from your page, be sure to tag the content designers involved.

Craft your pitch

For wider business areas that haven't yet grasped the fundamentals of content design, I suggest running workshops or presentations to teach the value of your work.

Before these sessions, think about the audience, their goals, and their motivations. Perhaps they're a legal team focused on making sure customers engage with their terms and conditions, or maybe they're a sales team focused on growing their customer base. Use the language of your audience when you present. For example, ecommerce people want to hear about leads and conversions, but legal folks might want to hear about comprehension and risk avoidance. Tailoring our language or format to reflect the audience is a tactic we employ for customer-facing content, but one we often forget when it comes to internal-facing content. I spoke with Kristina Halvorson, who has worked with many companies over the years and knows what it takes to get the right people engaged:

> *When you need other teams or leadership to "get" the importance (and complexity) of getting content right, the best thing you can do is essentially craft a sales pitch tailored to whatever pain points they're currently suffering—and show, don't tell. If you can connect better content to better outcomes in their particular job area, light bulbs will start to go off!*

Position the workshop as an educational session showing how content design can be used to create user-centered content and solve business problems. Explain that whatever the attendee's role—everyone creates content, even if it's just writing emails—they'll gain expertise from content designers who are willing to share. Set the context of why good content matters, with high-level intros on:

- **Accessibility:** Every company needs to think about how to ensure that their products, services, and communications are accessible to everyone.
- **Relevance:** Whatever a business needs to do or wants to say has to be positioned in a way that's relevant to users in the moment. This is something that crosses into all areas of a business, such as call center scripts and customer marketing emails.
- **Connecting content:** All content should be underpinned by a shared set of values, principles, voice, and terminology. Connected and well-crafted content helps customers trust a brand. Share a high-level map to demonstrate how many different types of content need to connect within your organization (**FIG 7.3**).
- **Consistency:** While the brand team might have established the brand voice, there's often confusion over how to adapt it for different scenarios (such as a critical error message). Content designers will maintain the consistency of voice but help adopt the appropriate tone for the occasion.
- **Clarity and brevity:** Content designers are able to crystallize concepts in just a few words. They can teach the whole company how to turn complex key messages into something short and snappy.
- **Being human:** Almost all businesses could be better at using simple, inclusive language; avoiding jargon; and focusing on human outcomes. Teaching other teams how to do this is another way to add value outside of day-to-day product work.

Share specific examples that bring these points to life or, even better, include some interactive exercises and end with suggestions for how you could collaborate more closely in the future to help teams reach their specific goals. Once people realize how much they need the expertise of content design, they're more likely to embrace it.

CUSTOMER GOAL	CUSTOMER-FACING CONTENT
Research and consider	• Marketing and advertising • Social media • Product/app descriptions • In-store merchandising • Printed content • Site navigation • Site architecture • Articles/blogs
Buy/join/commit	• Online forms • Purchase interface • Product descriptions • Legal wording, terms and conditions • App store listings • Emails • Call center/retail conversations
Fix problem/get help	• SMS • Call center/support conversations • Emails • Notifications • Help content • Site architecture • Live chat • Navigation labels • Printed content • Social media
Rebuy/renew/advocate	• Site architecture • Navigation labels • Online forms • Renewal interface • Call center/retail conversations • Emails • SMS • Notifications

FIG 7.3: There are many different content types across an organization's journey phases. This can often be eye-opening for teams who don't yet value the role of content.

INTERNAL-FACING CONTENT	BUSINESS GOAL
• Brand values • Tone of voice • Product naming and terminology • Content modeling/CMS structure	Attract
• Call center scripts/retail conversation guides • Product naming and terminology • Marketing propositions/mission statements • CMS interface messaging • Content design system	Convert and acquire
• Call center scripts/support conversation guides • Internal process interfaces • Live chat scripts • Propositions	Service and build relationship
• Call center scripts/retail conversation guides • Incentives • Internal process interfaces	Encourage loyalty

Building your content brand

After the immediate education, cultivating your cross-functional relationships is vital. This outreach and relationship-building can take up much of the job, but it reaps immense rewards. It relies on outreach to provide a clear, ongoing articulation of:

- the work your team is doing,
- its value to the organization, and
- how your team is helping others to achieve their goals.

There are many different and engaging ways to show your work. Use your content design community to decide on the most appropriate methods for the people you need to influence, and decide on the frequency of each activity. While we've touched on many methods and activities for outreach in this and previous chapters, there are several others to consider.

Weekly roundups

Encourage your content community to share content work and inspiration around the business. Newsletter emails and dashboards posts are great formats for sharing weekly roundups of content-related information. In *Cultivating Content Design*, Beth Dunn makes the excellent point that a well-written newsletter can make people realize your team "has something they want."

Things you might share:

- Inspiring examples from outside brands or industries
- Articles from content thought leaders
- Useful resources: Content Design London has a whole wiki on the value of content design (https://bkaprt.com/lcd41/07-02/) and their readability guidelines are useful (https://bkaprt.com/lcd41/07-03/)
- Positive results from split testing you've done
- A visual dashboard that communicates progress against your metrics (your analytics team members are great allies when it comes to creating dashboards or charts that help bring results to life)

- Blog posts with top content tips
- Profiles of the content team or "day in the life" articles
- Interviews with people in related content functions (they'll feel flattered and included)

Case studies

If your team has big results from a content project, they should share them. We're often bad at promoting ourselves, but it's a key part of influencing. Backed by the rigor of research, learning, and iteration, your team has a strong story to tell. Give them a simple template to create case studies:

- **A compelling title and intro.** Start with the outcome in the intro and then return to it at the end. This is a great way to illustrate impact.
- **The context.** Explain the project background and how the work came about.
- **Research summary.** How did the team understand more about the problem?
- **The key insights.** What new problems and opportunities did the team identify? Include any key artifacts such as experience maps. Demonstrate collaborative work through workshop photos or screenshots of virtual boards.
- **The hypothesis.** What did the team determine was the best solution and why? What impact did they hope to have? Include any success metrics.
- **The design process.** What did the team do? How did they test, iterate, and implement their ideas? If ideas were prototyped and tested, include images of the prototypes.
- **The outcome.** What were the results? How will this work inform future developments? What did the team learn by going through the process? Include any testimonials or feedback to enrich the story further.

Case studies don't just create good-news stories to share; they also provide something others can learn from. (I've even seen case studies turned into short videos that really bring a project to life for other teams.) Use them to share outcomes, whether good or bad; the lessons will help teams avoid repeating mistakes.

Open events

There are many opportunities to invite stakeholders and colleagues to participate in content-centered events. Consider:

- Running writing workshops for people in the business who like to write copy but have no formal training. It's amazing how much they realize they don't know when they spend a day with experts.
- Hosting lunch-and-learn sessions as bite-size opportunities to teach others about content designers and their methods. You can focus on specific content techniques or run a shorter, more informal version of the educational stakeholder workshops.
- Inviting those outside your design team to attend crit sessions. Better still, hold crits in an open area where other teams can see what's happening or can stop by to watch.
- Putting together roadshows or "science fairs" to showcase your work across the company. These will educate people about your initiatives and allow you to demonstrate success.

Andy Welfle, coauthor of *Writing is Designing,* told me about his annual "socialization tour" at Adobe:

I schedule a little time with stakeholders around the company and just talk about the team's goals, accomplishments, and growth over the last year. We share case studies of successes and our strategic goals to get feedback and to keep people in the loop. I try to hit up every design director, most of the design managers, several product leaders, and some partners in, say, localization, marketing, and brand. It's a lot, but it's really useful to bring people on a journey with me.

Whatever events you try, use them to share real examples from your team's work or learnings from projects (even when they didn't quite go as planned).

Working walls

To help show how rigorous content design can be, it can really help to show your work. Designers have been doing this forever—sharing their design explorations and how they came to a solution. In *Writing Is Design*, Andy Welfle and Michael Metts echo this sentiment: "One thing visual designers figure out pretty quickly is that the visual aspect of their work is powerful. As a writer, you should leverage that power."

Make your new workflows, tools, and frameworks visible to the whole team (and key stakeholders), so they understand content designers' working methods and the overarching steps to creating good content. Create a visual representation of your team's work near a high-traffic area. You might choose to pin up current customer experience maps, conversation journeys, or research outputs. Make sure the work is continually updated—add sticky notes of recommendations, iterations, or copy explorations. Encourage product teams to use this space for workshopping or crits. Let stakeholders stop by and ask questions.

Once senior leadership sees the workings behind the content and understands there's a process and rigor behind it, they begin to realize it's a whole lot more than "just words" and that it's pretty hard to do well.

GET OUT THERE AND MAKE YOURSELVES KNOWN

It can sometimes feel demoralizing when you're trying to build a team and create advocates—it's like you're pushing water uphill. The truth is that in most big organizations, you'll come up against doubters or those who put obstacles in your way.

You can have the best vision statement, the most efficient tools, and a smoothly laid-out process, but when it comes to building your team's brand, you need to invest time in doing outreach, creating high-level allies, and managing upward and outward.

I buy into the philosophy of doing one small thing each day that moves you closer to your goal. Whether that's setting up a lunch-and-learn or giving a content designer the confidence to challenge design decisions, there's always something you can do to incrementally improve the perception of content design. The trick is not to give up when you face a setback. Resilience is the key to moving the discipline forward, and the key to making each collaborative project even better than the last.

CONCLUSION

IF YOU'VE MADE IT THIS FAR, it's because you genuinely care about helping your team grow and make an impact—both on the experiences they're creating and on the business.

You'll also realize how much of leadership is operational, and how worthwhile it is to have someone dedicated to ops work. Perhaps you can use this book to convince your leadership team to invest in ops.

You may have found that some of these tools, tips, and techniques resonate more than others, and you're keen to try some of them right away. Before jumping in, remember to do your research to find out which one will provide the most value to your team. It might be one you hadn't even considered!

After your first success, you'll be hungry for more. Bit by bit, you'll notice improvements and increased effectiveness as you help your team become more mature. One of the most rewarding parts of doing this work is helping content teams get unstuck and start to thrive.

That said, ops work is never finished. Those doing design work will always need help removing barriers, building advocacy and capability, and continuously improving. But once you hit your stride with it, these tasks become a lot easier.

I wrote this book to share what I've learned as I've tried to break down complex problems and make sense of the operational side of leadership. I hope this book helps you make sense of operations, too—and helps you scale your team with lasting impact.

ACKNOWLEDGMENTS

I'D LIKE TO START by saying thank you to all the great content strategists and design leaders who inspired me to try many of the techniques mentioned in this book. While I may have used many of them in different content roles for different purposes, moving into ops allowed me to pull all these techniques together and make much more sense of them.

I am also hugely grateful to all the people who inspired me to write content books in the first place. My shelf is filled with too many to list, but they include the likes of Ginny Redish, Kristina Halvorson and Melissa Rach, Sara Wachter-Boettcher, Nicole Fenton and Kate Kiefer-Lee, Torrey Podmajerksy, Meghan Casey, Michael Metts and Andy Welfle, Carrie Hane, Sarah Winters, and Beth Dunn. I have quoted many of them in this book.

A special thank-you to Sara Wachter-Boettcher, who encouraged me to speak to A Book Apart, and an even bigger thank you to the team there who took a chance on me. The (quite frankly miraculous) editing skills of Lisa Maria Marquis turned my stream of consciousness into an actual book, and Adaobi Obi Tulton and Susan Bond also helped me fine-tune the content into something readable.

Thank you from the bottom of my heart to the following people who provided input to this book and made it so much better: Sarah Winters, Jonathon Colman, Hilary Marsh, Sara Wachter-Boettcher, Andy Welfle, Candi Williams, Jess Sattell, Torrey Podmajersky, and Amy Thibodeau. And a huge thank you to Frances Whinder and Kimberley Porter for giving up their time to review the manuscript and provide valuable feedback.

Thank you to my fellow content designers for keeping me going and making our community such a joyous place.

And lastly, thank you to Martyn Reding for always being my number-one cheerleader and supporting me throughout, and to my amazing children, Finton and Felix, for putting up with months of neglect while I wrote this book—you can have your dinner now!

RESOURCES

I'VE READ QUITE A FEW content books and articles throughout my career, but a few have stuck with me (some of which I've already mentioned). Here's my pick of the most helpful—the ones you'll dip back into again and again as you shape and grow your team and its capability:

- *Content Design* by Sarah Winters. A classic introduction to content design and a great guide for identifying user needs (https://bkaprt.com/lcd41/08-01/).
- *The Content Strategy Toolkit* by Meghan Casey. This book was ahead of its time, with many great tools and templates for everything from sitemaps to prioritization (https://bkaprt.com/lcd41/08-02/).
- *Content Strategy for the Web* by Kristina Halvorson and Melissa Rach. One of the first books I read about content strategy, and still one to refer back to all these years later, with great tips for advocacy, too.
- *Content Everywhere* by Sara Wachter-Boettcher. A must-read for anyone looking to systematize their content. Again, a classic that's still relevant today (https://bkaprt.com/lcd41/08-03/).
- *Strategic Writing for UX* by Torrey Podmajersky. There are some great techniques in Torrey's book, and I always recommend it to both designers and content designers, particularly for the conversational design exercise (https://bkaprt.com/lcd41/08-04/).
- *Writing Is Designing* by Michael Metts and Andy Welfle. Full disclosure, I was a technical reviewer for this one—but it's great, bringing content design to life in such a brilliant, down-to-earth way (https://bkaprt.com/lcd41/08-05/).
- *Cultivating Content Design* by Beth Dunn. Beth provides excellent tips for building content advocacy in this well-written and easy-to-read book (https://bkaprt.com/lcd41/08-06/).

- *Nicely Said* by Nicole Fenton and Kate Kiefer-Lee. Over the years, this book really helped me bring marketing teams on board with some of the proposition exercises (https://bkaprt.com/lcd41/08-07/).
- *How to Make Sense of Any Mess* by Abby Covert. A great little intro to the importance of information architecture. Abby has also created a wonderful heuristics framework that can be used as prompt for IA projects or content audits. You can even buy a poster from her Etsy store (https://bkaprt.com/lcd41/08-08/)!
- *Designing Connected Content* by Mike Atherton and Carrie Hane. A must-read for those who want to get started in content modeling, with some clear guidance on creating structured content (https://bkaprt.com/lcd41/08-09/).
- *Resilient Management* by Lara Hogan. Lara shares great tips and techniques for managing people, such as providing constructive feedback and developing a team vision (https://bkaprt.com/lcd41/08-10/).
- *The Making of a Manager* by Julie Zhou. A simple how-to guide for building relationships with your team members and having effective conversations (https://bkaprt.com/lcd41/08-11/).
- *Radical Candor* by Kim Scott. A book that inspires confidence for having challenging conversations and managing tricky stakeholders (https://bkaprt.com/lcd41/08-12/).
- "How to define content principles for your team" by Lauren Pope. A helpful article on Gather Content (which has a whole host of wonderful articles) to help you create your team commandments (https://bkaprt.com/lcd41/08-13/).

REFERENCES

Shortened URLs are numbered sequentially; the related long URLs are listed below for reference.

Chapter 7

07-01 https://www.pechakucha.com/

07-02 https://contentdesign.london/content-design/value-of-content-design/

07-03 https://readabilityguidelines.co.uk

Resources

08-01 https://contentdesign.london/store/the-content-design-book/

08-02 https://www.dobettercontent.com

08-03 https://rosenfeldmedia.com/books/content-everywhere/

08-04 https://torreypodmajersky.com/strategic-writing-for-ux/

08-05 https://www.writingisdesigning.com

08-06 https://abookapart.com/products/cultivating-content-design

08-07 http://www.nicelysaid.co

08-08 https://www.etsy.com/shop/abbytheia

08-09 https://www.pearson.com/us/higher-education/program/Hane-De-signing-Connected-Content-Plan-and-Model-Digital-Products-for-To-day-and-Tomorrow/PGM1816611.html

08-10 https://abookapart.com/products/resilient-management

08-11 https://www.juliezhuo.com/book/manager.html

08-12 https://www.radicalcandor.com/the-book/

08-13 https://gathercontent.com/blog/how-to-define-content-principles-for-your-team

INDEX

A

assessing Tools 57-60
auditing frameworks 76

B

building your team 40-47

C

camaraderie 92-93
Casey, Meghan 31
collective capability 37-40
Colman, Jonathon 9
community of practice 111
considering design systems 79-83
content designers 2
content management system (CMS) 2
content managers 2
content models 73-75
content operations, defined 7
content request visibility 63-64
content responsibilities 51-52
content trap 5-7
conversational ideation workshop 95
creating a content team vision 44-47
customer experience mapping 53-54

D

defining standards 71-79
design cycle 16-17
developing skillsets 41-43
dot-voting 25
Dunn, Beth 18, 21, 57, 128

E

ecosystem mapping 49-51

F

facilitation skills 116

G

governing standards 86-87

H

Halvorson, 7
Halvorson, Kristina 124
Hogan, Lara 113

I

ideation 25-28
identifying allies 21-22
individual capability 33-37
individual contributors (ICs) 34
influencing organizational change
      61-68
interviews 18-19

J

job shadowing 21

K

key performance indicators (KPIs) 29

M

managing standards 84-86
measuring success 29-31
meeting observation 21
messaging matrices 72-73
Metts, Michael 64, 131
minimum viable product (MVP) 28

P

pair-writing practices 66-67
Perez-Cruz, Yesenia 80, 86
Podmajersky, Torrey 63, 70, 86, 95
premortems 98
problem definition 22-24
project framework 93-94
prototyping and testing 28-29

R

RACI chart 52
red-amber-green (RAG) rating 78
research and discovery 17-22
roadmapping 26
role expectations 34-35

S

Sattell, Jess 71, 81, 85
Spencer, Donna 107, 116
stakeholder management 102-109
    feedback 108-109
    mapping 103-104
    presentations 106-108
    research involvment 104-105
standardizing content hand-offs 65-66
strategy and operations 13-15
streamlining workflows 55-57

T

tasks 8-9
teaching other teams 121-123
team structures 10-12
team trust and health 91-92
testing templates 75
Thibodeau, Amy 81, 87
time-tracking surveys 19-20
tool governance 60

W

Wachter-Boettcher, Sara 78
Webber, Emily 111
Welfle, Andy 64, 90, 130, 131
Williams, Candi 112
Winters, Sarah 66, 110, 112
working with development Teams
    99-102
working with product teams 90-98

Z

Zhou, Julie 45

ABOUT A BOOK APART

We cover the emerging and essential topics in web design and development with style, clarity, and above all, brevity—because working designer-developers can't afford to waste time.

COLOPHON

The text is set in FF Yoga and its companion, FF Yoga Sans, both by Xavier Dupré. Headlines and cover are set in Titling Gothic by David Berlow.

 This book was printed in the United States using FSC certified papers.

FSC
www.fsc.org